The Art Of Metaphysical Communication

Conversations With The Other Side

Howard F. Batie
with
The Spiritual Research Group

It is good to be a seeker,
But sooner or later, you must become a finder.
And then it is good to give what you have found,
A gift into the world for whoever will accept it

-Richard Bach in
Jonathan Livingston Seagull

First Edition
Copyright © 2018
All Rights Reserved
ISBN-10: 1727341465
ISBN-13: 978-1727341461
CreateSpace Independent Publishing Platform,
North Charleston, SC 29406, USA

Table of Contents

About the Front Cover -

Entura Art Reading (See Chapter 1) 1997 Chalk Drawing by Patricia Hayes, Co-Founder of Delphi University (www.delphiu.com) and Developer of Entura Art. In an expanded state of awareness, Patricia drew this picture of what she 'saw' in the author's energy field. When the drawing was completed, she returned to full conscious awareness and discussed each element of the picture, as given in the following extract of the session transcript.

When I first look at a picture, usually one thing catches my attention. But in this one, everything catches my attention! But I'm going to start with the gold sun because this sun is a manifestation of the spiritual sun shining in you, and there is a (crescent) array of five stars coming into it. This is significant because it represents the five areas of your mission, and when you decided to come this time from the Pleiades, you had a great clarity of why you were going to come.

You work with a very large group, and I want to call it a brotherhood. The star closest to the sun is your ability to heal the physical body, and the second star will be your healing of the etheric body. The Third star represents your emotional and mental connections, and the fourth star represents your energization of spirit with the people you work with. The last star is your ability to communicate, which enables the writings that will come through you. First, you will touch their mind, but by the end of the book, their hearts will also be touched. So, it will be written with purpose like an opera that begins on one level, then intensifies and builds until the end, which is the drama, the touching of the soul. At the top of the arc with five stars is a dolphin, which is a symbol of communication, and being in the heavens, means that your writings will come from your soul. The written word is really what you are to leave behind. It's your legacy, it's why you are here.

To the left is an enormous Archangelic presence that guides your work; its mouth is open to speak often with you, and its heart is full of light and radiantly open. Below is a group of Scribes who have already prepared your written messages – your job is to just bring them through. To the right of the sun is your primary healing physician and a host of other Angelic helpers who can be called upon if needed. The 'raindrops' falling from the sun are energizing your heart and falling to the water below, which represents the unconscious mind. The raindrops and the spiritual healers are leading another dolphin on the water, which represents communicating your message to the masses, and the lotus blossoms are the awakenings that will happen in many places.

Lastly, but very important for you, is the true heart love that will very soon come into your life. [I was divorced and living alone at the time.] *This is the wedding of your spiritual self and her spiritual self, and behind you are the wings that represent the freedom for both of you that will come from this union. This love will enhance your writings and give it new dimensions.* [We were married in 2000.)

vi

Acknowledgements

This book has been made possible through the continuing dedication and support my many Hypnotherapy and Energy Healing clients who have come together to support each other in our monthly Spiritual Discussion Group (see Appendix A). Several dozen clients have steadfastly progressed through the development of the Spiritual Journeys Program, volunteered to become the initial members of our Spiritual Research Group for exploring previously unknown areas of their awareness, and learned to interact and converse with their own Higher Selves and Spirit Guides. With their ability to access their own personal Akashic Records, they have become experienced Channels for the higher wisdom of the Ascended Masters and the Angelic Kingdom, and I sincerely thank each and each one of you for your continued friendship, comradery and patience. This book is as much your story as it is mine.

In addition, I send much gratitude and love to those very special persons who have been there for me throughout my own Journey, especially for my loving wife Anita and her constant encouragement and caring support for me every step of the way, I will always treasure you and your love.

To Dottie Graham, my first spiritual mentor, I send my everlasting thanks for your inspirational guidance and patience with this left-brained engineer! I will always treasure your bright and optimistic attitude, and your workshops that introduced me to the metaphysical world. Your Healing Sanctuaries resonated strongly and deeply within me and taught me how to step out and become an instrument of healing for others.

For August Armstrong who first allowed me a personal glimpse into my own past lives, a very special Thank You! The information you provided was so accurate and your encouragement so strong, all doubt about this fascinating new ability to tap into "external" information was erased.

For Patricia Hayes, Marshall Smith, Kimberley, Charles, Janice and all the extraordinary teachers at Delphi University, the smorgasbord of spiritual classes and topics there provided a very strong foundation upon which I would build a new life for myself as a spiritual healing facilitator and teacher. And special thanks to Patricia Hayes for the wonderful front cover Entura Art chalk drawing.

For Dr. Henry Kirk, as past President of Centralia College when I returned to the area where I grew up, your encouragement for me to offer energy healing classes through the College's Continuing Education Department resulted in a roomful of students who asked to be my first clients. Thank you! The opportunity you provided me resulted in my establishing the Evergreen Healing Arts Center, which has provided a wide array of energy healing and Hypnotherapy services to our local community for over two decades.

And to each and every one of my clients over the last 22 years, I send a huge Thank You as well. It was only because of your continuing trust and patronage that I was able to learn so much through the experience of working with you. There is a great and wonderful synergy between student and teacher, and neither can be effective without the other!

Foreword

I remember the moment I met Howard Batie.

It was in 2005 at a training for Life Between Lives in Boulder, Colorado. We were students in that course together, and I was drawn to Howard during one of the breaks. What struck me immediately was his warmth and his wisdom. I felt like I was talking to my favourite uncle at a family reunion and there was a rare mix of passion, gentleness and something else that I can now more readily put my finger on. Here was a man who wanted to make a difference to humanity.

Spiritual teachers come in many guises. From people like the Dalai Lama or Mother Theresa, all the way through to the local bus driver or the gardener at the local spiritual centre, these people carry a few basic characteristics that makes them spiritual teachers.

Firstly, their life's work is simply an offering. It comes from their experiences in life and reflects a deeper wisdom, rather than simply the passing on of doctrine and philosophies that have been inherited over time. They breathe new life into the old ways. They are here to herald a new awakening for humanity in their own way, whether it be touching the hearts of a large gathering, or that of a single soul in a life changing conversation.

Secondly, they are part of something greater than themselves, and they stand boldly in the energy of service as they offer that in a way that transcends ego – that great affliction of so many of our species. Spiritual teachers understand that the consciousness of the group takes care of the individual identities within that group. They advocate oneness as a way to solve the issues of this world and beyond.

Finally, they offer what they do with humility and humour, as a gentle offering of service for a greater cause.

For my mind, Howard Batie is a spiritual teacher as he holds the energy of these three characteristics. But in Howard there is more...

I have no doubt that what he brings to humanity has emerged more fully from the path he chose along the way. With the discipline of military service, blended with a finely tuned engineering brain, he is well balanced with the experience of being an NDE survivor and the energy of the spiritual explorer. Howard brings an eclectic mix of robust research in a multidimensional universe where the metaphysical meets the practical to offer something of deep insight to humanity.

I have watched Howard's work emerge over many years, and for me it has always manifested into something of great importance at precisely the right time, as humanity is now wrestling with the concept of the evolution of our collective consciousness to a new state of being.

When Howard published his book, *The ETs Speak: Who We Are And Why We're Here,* something happened for me as I sat at my computer and his simple email about the book dropped into my inbox. I felt the importance of that book and the messages contained therein. I contacted Howard immediately and soon afterwards, asked him to speak at the World Conference for The Michael Newton Institute for Life Between Lives Hypnotherapy. Having done my own research into expanded states and other realities, I just knew in my heart that Howard was on to something. When he was unable to attend due to his health, we "virtualised" him and got him there anyway.

There is a great deal in this book and, as Howard says, take what resonates for you. It is rare indeed to find such a smorgasbord of metaphysical information. I encourage you to read the pages that follow with an open mind and an open heart, as there is something here for everyone. How much so is, of course, up to you.

In closing, I'd like to offer my own reflection and it is quite simple, really.

If there were more Howard Baties on this earth, then humanity would be further along the path of evolution, and this world would be a better place.

I believe you will enjoy *The Art of Metaphysical Communication*.

Peter Smith, August 10, 2018
President, The Michael Newton Institute for LBL Hypnotherapy,
Founder, Institute for Quantum Consciousness,
Author, *Quantum Consciousness: Journey through other realms*

Introduction

The information provided in this book may include new or unfamiliar concepts that could conflict with previously held truths already held as a part of your personal belief system. This book provides information about many of the modalities and techniques that I have been trained and certified in, and have found to be very helpful over more than twenty years, both as an Energy Healing Practitioner (Reiki, Healing Touch, Theta Healing, etc.) and as a Certified and Registered Hypnotherapist. Through their application, I have been able to assist my clients to increase their health and wellness and to interact in a positive and loving way with others. If the topics and modalities discussed herein are of interest to you, you may want to investigate those that you feel comfortable with; if not, feel free to pass this book to another who might be more comfortable with the material.

Validation versus Proof

As a Lifelong Learner, I never run out of interesting information and ideas to explore, and am willing to consider, at least for a short time, any topic or idea from the hard scientific areas to the more speculative or fantastic concepts of science fiction. However, I also like to believe that I can discern the validity of concepts and information in between these opposite genres. My own personal Validity Scale runs from zero to ten, with a score of zero representing information that is neither valid nor included in my world view of reality at all; on the other end of the scale, the things that I <u>know</u> are true and I can always count on, receive a score of 10. In between is that gray area which holds all the things I'm not sure about, and are hard for me to call "True," but which might be interesting to investigate "someday."

In most Western civilizations, the truth of information is determined either through the objective scientific method or through subjective personal experience. After forming a theory or belief about an event or process, the scientist will attempt to prove the theory is true or untrue using the scientific method (repeated empirical measurements under controlled conditions). However, this scientific method falls short of being able validate the personal experience of a metaphysical event, for instance, a Near-Death Experience (NDE), a true déja vu experience, or a sudden 'knowing' that something is true without knowing where that thought came from. That metaphysical event may be investigated and validated as true, but only for the person who actually experienced the event. The point here is that there is a big difference between a global objective Truth and the personal validity of an event that has been subjectively experienced.

Much of the information presented in this book is the result of my personal experiences that have helped to form a coherent understanding of my expanding belief system and reality. However, you will need to decide the validity of the information presented here and its relevance to your own belief system (things that you hold to be true), which may be different from the belief systems of others.

Background

Looking back at my lifetime, this book is as much about the many modalities and types of "Communication" that I have learned, explored, and become familiar with, as it is about the series of serendipitous so-called 'coincidences' that have provided the major theme of "Communications" as my pathway throughout my life's Journey.

My early childhood in Centralia, Washington was a happy idyllic time of innocent playfulness and wonder at all the new things in my small world – my own little tricycle, building imaginary forts in the open field behind our house, playing Cowboys and Indians with my brothers and neighbors, catching lightning bugs in a glass pint jar in the summer, and all the other little-boy activities we enjoyed. And then, when I was about nine or ten years old, I remember hearing very clearly, "Well, now that you're here, you'd better learn how to fit in with all those other people!" That felt very odd, and my next thought was, "Now where did THAT come from?" Nobody was there to answer, so I just kept on playing.

Later that year, my family would drive several hours to the home of my grandparents in Seattle for festive holidays such as Thanksgiving and Christmas. On one of those visits, I asked my grandmother about the picture of a mountain that she had hanging in her kitchen. It was a great mountain that grew up out of a peaceful valley to majestically high peaks covered with snow, and I wanted to know if it was nearby Mt. Rainier. She said, "No, that is just a picture of Life. There are a thousand paths up the mountain, but they all lead to the same place. It does not really matter which path you choose, but CHOOSE ONE and START WALKING!" Good advice, but it was several years later in 1985 that I really started walking on my own path.

Many times, during my childhood and adult life, I would occasionally hear what I came to call 'The Voice' that gave me a short message, or even just a single word (usually "NO!"). I learned through the School of Hard Knocks that whenever I listened to The Voice and took its advice, good things happened; but when I ignored the advice and did things My Way, usually emotional or financial disaster quickly followed. As a result, I soon came to regard The Voice as a helpful friend and mentor, upon whom I could rely for positive guidance.

During my early High School years, I became interested in ham radio, and learned Morse Code with another classmate; we took the exam together, received our licenses, and 'talked' with many friends from around the world. After graduating from High School, I graduated from the University of Washington in 1962 from the School of Communications and the next day was commissioned as an Ensign in the Navy. A month later, I reported to my ship, which was homeported in San Francisco, and was assigned to be the Communications Officer, along with several additional junior officer duties. My shipboard life was very full and very busy as we made the first of two six-month tours to the Western Pacific in the initial campaigns of the Vietnam War.

After a short duty assignment in Scotland from 1964-1965, I accepted an offer to attend the US Naval Postgraduate School in Monterey, California and became a member of the first graduating class in Communications Systems Management, earning a subspecialty code for "Communications Management." Following another three-year shipboard tour as Operations Officer during the height of the Viet Nam War, and as a result of my Communications Management code, in 1970 I was assigned to the office of the Director for Naval Communications in the Pentagon. My first duty there was, with nine other officers and experienced radiomen, to develop the first operational concept for a geostationary satellite communications architecture that could support all the operational, technical and support requirements of surface, submarine and airborne Naval forces world-wide. It was also my job to provide the technical support information to the Admirals who would petition Congress to fund this much more capable communication system. The Navy really did need to replace the Morse Code, Teletype and High Frequency radio systems that were still in use, simply because they were unreliable at long oceanic distances.

During this time, I continued my ham radio hobby, constructed much of my own electronic communication equipment, and published more than 26 magazine articles in the emerging consumer electronics and computer fields. I also designed and constructed a personal computer system to help severely physically handicapped Cerebral Palsy patients communicate with their family, and a description of the system was published in a special supplement to the Journal of International Electrical and Electronics Engineers. In addition, I designed and constructed a solar-powered telemetry system for the US Geological Survey to provide an improved monitoring capability at several volcanos around the world. Seven such monitoring systems were vaporized when Mt. St. Helens erupted in Washington State in 1980.

In 1982, after a total of 20-years' service, I retired as a Lieutenant Commander, and then remained in the suburbs of Washington, DC to continue climbing the corporate ladder of companies in the area that provide Systems Engineering and Technical Assistance (SETA) in support of military satellite communications and other overhead programs. However, in January 1995, I received another very strong audible message from 'The Voice' that changed my life. It shouted loudly in my mind, "Howard, it's time!" In the same instant, I somehow "knew" that it was time for me to move out of the technical military world and relocate to Virginia Beach, Virginia, a place that I had no previous ties to. There was also a sense of urgency in the very direct message given by The Voice, and I consciously made a life-changing decision to follow this inner guidance without really knowing where it might lead: I went into work that morning, told my Vice-President that I quit my job, put my house on the market, and began packing my belongings in preparation for what I felt was to be the adventure of a lifetime.

Three months later I found myself in Virginia Beach, which is the host to two very different groups of people: one seasonal and one year-round. In the summer months the beautiful beaches attract the sunbathing, surfing, and beach-combing vacationers who follow the sun and warmth of summer. But Virginia Beach is also a year-round focal point for a very large and active metaphysical community. As home to the Association for Research and Enlightenment, and the Edgar Cayce Foundation, this area is also noted for attracting a wide variety of psychics, Tarot card readers, energy healers, astrologers, and for providing instructional workshops to train practitioners of nearly every alternative healing technique or practice.

Soon after relocating to nearby Chesapeake, VA, and wondering why I was there, I was introduced to a wide variety of energy healing techniques – an area that I had not even heard about before, much less considered joining. I received several flyers in the mail that said I could learn to become a Reiki Healer. My initial reaction was rejection of that "woo-woo stuff," but my curiosity eventually got the better of my skepticism, and I responded to one of the fliers for a short introductory Reiki session "just to feel its energies." During the short session, the belief system of my logical linear, well-ordered left-brain was shattered completely. I physically felt a twisting in my Solar Plexus and "saw" in my mind a tight knot in a huge rope unwind and straighten out. When I asked the Reiki Master what it all meant, she said simply, "I don't know – I didn't feel or see anything. What does it mean to YOU?" Unable to answer or even get my mind around what I had physically felt, I decided that I would have to learn to provide Reiki in order to understand what I had experienced in this physical and visual experience. That was another turning point for me. My linear, thinking, engineering mind could not even begin to comprehend what I had obviously felt and sensed physically, so I began learning about this new metaphysical world by paying attention to what I was experiencing and feeling.

After becoming a Reiki Practitioner, I began providing Reiki sessions to clients, and also attended several workshops for other energy healing modalities as well, including Breathwork, Healing Touch, Healing With Color And Sound, and several others. In addition, I attended interesting workshops and individual sessions in Astrology, Tarot Cards, Psychic Readings, and many different meditation techniques. Along this fascinating new pathway, I even attended a wonderful Spiritual Healing Sanctuary as a recipient of spiritual healing energies, and Dr. Dottie Graham, the Sanctuary leader, soon agreed to mentor me in a wider range of physical and energetic healing techniques.

One of these techniques that she introduced to me was Ro-Hun, an energy healing technique designed to release all the major emotional blocks that are holding a person back from fully expressing the fullness and love of who and what they really are. The Ro-Hun process is extensively described and discussed in my 2003 book, *"Healing Body. Mind & Spirit,"* as well as Janice Hayes' 2013 book, *"Ro-Hun Therapy: The*

Greatest Transformational Process of Our Time." In a manner similar to many other healing techniques, the Ro-Hun processes are learned most effectively by directly experiencing them first-hand as a client before learning to provide the processes to others.

Following my Ro-Hun training, I found that I was much better prepared to assist my clients in releasing their emotional blocks and negative or limiting beliefs about themselves and others. As they told their friends and acquaintances about the new and positive changes in their own lives, my Ro-Hun practice significantly expanded to the point where I no longer needed to advertise – my clients were doing that for me! Although I was only using energetic techniques to facilitate these Ro-Hun sessions, I recognized that I was in fact facilitating Past Life Regressions (PLRs) that would otherwise require the practitioner to be a Certified Hypnotherapist; therefore, I soon became Certified in Hypnotherapy as well, and added an expanded array of hypnotherapeutic techniques for assisting with my clients' physical and emotional issues.

In 1998, I moved back to Southwest Washington State where I grew up and opened my energy healing and hypnotherapy practice, Evergreen Healing Arts Center, in Chehalis, WA. There, my practice continued to expand, and I also began providing workshops and instruction in the Inner Light Consciousness Meditation technique that I had learned while in Virginia. This meditation technique was the only one of about twenty techniques I had tried that worked for my linear engineering mind, and I found that it also helped many others, ranging from engineers to artists, and from carpenters to musicians. Assisting others to attain altered states of higher consciousness seemed to come readily for me, and for my clients as well, and I decided to 'specialize' in the metaphysical development of my clients and exploration of these (for me) exciting new realms.

Definitions

So, this book you are now reading is really about some of the many forms of Metaphysical Communications that I explored during the life journey I have just outlined. To really understand this complex subject of metaphysical communication, including transformative healing experiences, first we need to define the terms that we will use. The first of these terms that we need to define is the word '**Metaphysical**' because 'metaphysical' means different things to different people. As it is being used in this book, the word 'metaphysical' simply means 'beyond the physical' and has no connection to or relationship with any religion or belief system. The next word to define is '**Communication**.' As is it being used in this book, 'Communication' is defined as the two-way exchange of information between a Sender and a Receiver. Therefore, for a human to be able to engage in 'Metaphysical Communication' means the establishment of a bi-directional pathway for exchange of information between a non-physical Sender and a physically human Receiver.

However, the eternal non-physical realm, where Guardian Angels, Spirit Guides and other non-physical beings exist, obviously operates with a different set of rules than we have here in this Physical Realm of existence that we call our day-to-day reality. This Metaphysical Model of Reality proposes that in the higher-dimensional non-physical realms of existence, beings are composed of only the energy of individual consciousness, there is no need for a physical body with a throat and voice to speak, and inter-personal communication is done by a telepathic exchange of energy packets, rather than ideas and thoughts wrapped in a spoken language. It is only in the lower Physical Realm of existence where humans exist that a voice and spoken language is needed to exchange information. This Metaphysical Model of Reality cannot be proven using rigorous scientific methods; however, the information provided in the continuing two-way discussions of our Channels with our non-physical spirit mentors have essentially validated the usefulness of this model for understanding the mechanisms and limitations of this mode of communication.

The term **Channel** also needs to be defined as it is being used in this book. A Channel is a human person who has been instructed in how to use a learned process to quickly (10-20 seconds or so) raise their consciousness into a state of greatly expanded awareness where they are able to contact and exchange information with a non-physical being. The Director of this process, usually a trained and experienced Certified Hypnotherapist, asks a question, and the Channel audibly provides the response to the question from the non-physical being's perspective, while remaining fully aware of both sides of the conversation. The process of conversing in a two-way dialogue with a spirit being is called **Channeling**. The general process for teaching the individual to be able to conversationally interact with the spirit being (but not the how-to steps) is described in my 2015 book, "*Spiritual Journeys: A Practical Methodology for Accelerated Spiritual Development and Experiential Exploration*". I refer to the group of Channels whom I have trained as our '**Spiritual Research Group**,' which is a subset of our Spiritual Discussion Group (see Appendix A).

The type of information that can be channeled is as varied as the questions that can be asked, with the primary restriction being that the answers must be in the greater good of all concerned. A channeling session may be held to receive personal guidance about what choice to make when faced with a fork in a pathway; however, the answers may not be direct. For instance, when facing a choice, the answer given may not be to choose A or B, but may be couched in terms of what choices A and B are each most likely to result in, leaving your choice open. Alternatively, the information received may provide additional insight into new healing abilities or techniques; previous events within our Universe may just as easily be reviewed. Our Spiritual Research Group has been told that as long as the answer is in the greater good of all concerned and will not cause harm to any being, any request for information will be honored.

Another term that needs to be defined is '**Spirit Being**'. As the Channels in our Spiritual Research Group began exploring the Spirit Realms (the area where only non-physical conscious beings exist), they were introduced to many forms of spirit beings, such as Angels, Spirit Guides, Ascended Masters and others described in Chapter 2. The common theme that nearly all Spirit Beings express is that they are, like us humans, also individually evolving in experience and wisdom as they follow their own path. Many spirit beings, such as Spirit Guides, Angels, and Archangels reportedly do not normally incarnate to experience physical reality for an entire physical lifetime; however, all conscious beings, spiritual or physical, are on their own pathway of increasing experience, wisdom and responsibility. Their infinite patience with us humans is also quite obvious, and it is quite reassuring that they are here to help us grow and learn, in the best way possible, to awaken to whom and what we really are, and to use our own thoughts and abilities responsibly.

The term '**Spiritual Area**' is also frequently mentioned in conjunction with the channeling process used by our Spiritual Research Group. The Spiritual Area is not a physical place; it is a greatly expanded state of consciousness where the individual Channel becomes aware of the beings and objects that are 'there' with them. It is an individual process that is experienced differently by each Channel; for one, they may see visual images of what they 'see' and for another it may be just a feeling that they are in the right place. For example, one of the Channels in our Spiritual Research Group can describe very clearly how her Spirit Guide appears to her, the color and design of her Guide's clothing, etc., and another Channel just "knows" she is in her Spiritual Area without any sensory input. And in contrast, I recognize the presence of my own Guide as a very strong and loving purple energy with a lot of swirling motion, yet each knows beyond a shadow of a doubt that we are in our own Guide's presence.

To illustrate the process of accessing our Spiritual Area, in our physical day-to-day existence, we need to remember that we are normally consciously aware only of what we have previously experienced through our five physical senses, usually after the age of about five or six when our personal consciousness (Ego) begins to develop and we become aware of ourselves as an independent and individual physical being. For us to be able to receive information from a spiritual being, we have to find a common area where we can expand our awareness to include a small portion of the Spiritual Realm, where we can meet and converse telepathically with the non-physical beings we wish to talk with. Referring to Figure 1 below, normally we are conscious only of our day-to-day physical reality, and Receiver A is not aware of the Spiritual Realm. But Receiver B has learned how to expand a portion of his or her consciousness into the lower levels of the Spirit Realm where a telepathic exchange of information between beings in the Physical and Spirit Realms is possible. I just call this area of Receiver B's expanded consciousness their 'Spiritual Area' where there is an intersection of receiver B's physical and non-physical realities. The Spiritual Journeys process is not the only method for accessing one's Spiritual Area; another method that does not require the use of hypnotherapeutic techniques is discussed in my 2017 book, *"Trans-Scalar Healing: Holistic Healing for Self, Others & Gaia."*

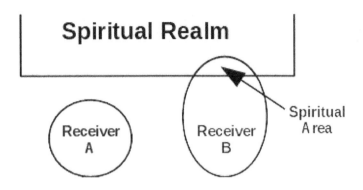

Figure 1. Spiritual Area Identified.

The Limitations Of Language

Now that we have identified "what" and "where" the Spiritual Area is, we need to understand the different ways that information can be transferred between the Spiritual and Physical Realms. Humans are capable of receiving information through their five primary physical senses, and each person has a preferred pathway for receiving this information, whether that is visually through their eyes, aurally through their ears, kinesthetically through their sense of feeling or touch, or, to a lesser degree, gustatorily through their sense of taste and olfactorily through their sense of smell. In addition, some have developed the beginnings of a "sixth sense" that allows them to intuitively "just know" that something is true for them; this is often known as "intuition."

For a moment, imagine that I wish to send to you the complete information and meaning of my experience when I hold a rose in my hand. I can attempt to describe to you how it looks and feels to me, but it is nearly impossible to fully describe in the language of words the sensations my fingers feel when I hold it in my hand, nor the shades and nuances of its colorations that I see, nor the infinite variety of the shape of its petals, nor the very vibrational essence of its aroma, nor the symbolic emotional and sentimental attachments that arise within me when I experience that rose. In other words, you, the Receiver, will be unable to receive the full experience of the rose that I enjoy. Further, every other person or Receiver will also have a different impression or experience of what 'a rose' means to them, and the full meaning will accordingly differ from one person to the next.

So, as you read a word on this page, your conscious mind has already translated the individual letter symbols that we have assigned to spoken sounds, and has formed them into larger symbols (words) in order to deduce the meaning or understanding of what I wish to convey. R-o-s-e becomes "rose" and even if you understand what "rose" means on one level, you will not enjoy the full meaning of what I intended to send to you. In addition, the *meaning* of the word 'rose' must be in the language and vocabulary of both Sender and Receiver in order to transfer meaning. This is the Limitation of Language that beings in the Spiritual Realm must somehow manage in order to communicate their information to humans in our language with more than an occasional energetic or intuitive 'nudge.' However, their desire to help, guide and inform us humans is unending, and many are willing to learn how to transmit their information to us in a way that we can understand.

Now that we begin to comprehend the extent of the difficulties in receiving information from the spiritual world, we need to also understand how a spiritual being normally exchanges information with and among other spirit beings. Obviously, non-physical beings do not have physical bodies with mouths and vocal cords, and are instead pure consciousness energy. In the many conversations that our Channels have had with several spirit beings, we have begun to understand that, without a physical body and a mouth, throat and voice to speak, the normal method for exchanging information between spirit beings is done through instantaneous exchange of energetic packets of information, intention and meaning. For instance, imagine that Spirit A wishes to send information to Spirit B; since they have no spoken language, this intention is instead instantly done telepathically by focusing Spirit A's attention on the vibrations and frequencies of Spirit B and intentionally and instantly sharing the desired information in an energetic 'package' consisting of visual imagery, conceptual ideas, motives, intentional objectives, symbols and colorful vibrations, coupled with their full meaning, feelings and emotions, in addition to simply factual understandings.

The entire breadth, depth and meaning of what "a rose" is to a spirit being is impossible to transfer to a human brain that is constrained by its physical nervous system and the limitations of language to express or share verbal information. Therefore, a Translator is essential for effective communication between a non-physical spiritual being – for example, between a Spirit Guide and a human Earthling. This Translator function is performed by what I call in this book, the **Higher Self**, a portion of the human's conscious soul essence. In our Metaphysical Model of Reality, the Higher Self is the portion of the **Soul** essence, the spark of Creator's energy, that closely identifies with a specific physical vehicle through the incarnation process. The purpose of the soul as an energetic spark of Creator is to explore and experience Creation in all its forms, gaining both knowledge and wisdom through its experiences and explorations. The purpose of the Higher Self is to experience and interact with its physical world and thereby add to the knowledge and wisdom of the Soul.

The soul's present experience is that of being incarnated into and integrated within a physical body and form (you) to experience and master the challenges of physicality, learning and growing through the language, culture and lessons that it has chosen for this entire physical lifetime. Therefore, as a non-physical consciousness that is also inhabiting and using both your physical body and the language your brain has learned, the Higher Self is the perfect Translator between purely spiritual beings and the human physical brain. The Higher Self then attempts to move the information received telepathically from the spiritual Sender through the linguistic and cultural filters that the brain has learned, so that it can express the spiritual information through the abilities of the physical body. This spiritual information may be expressed verbally as a 'channeled' message, visually as a drawn picture or painting, aurally as a beautiful musical score, kinesthetically as physical movements such as in a dance, or as a sculpture in clay, marble, or any other physical artistic medium or expressive modality that the person prefers. However, this process of working with a human and their Higher Self seems to still be a challenge for even highly evolved spirit beings, and they are very concerned that the information they wish to convey be clearly understood and comprehended by the human recipient. For example, during a verbal channeling session, they will often ask, "Is this clearly understood?" or "Am I being clear? Do you need clarification?"

Highlighted extracts from verbal transfers of information from a spiritual Sender (Guide, Angel, etc.) to a human Receiver (the

Channel), as facilitated by our Spiritual Research Group, are identified throughout this book with indented, italicized text as shown in the excerpt below (See Chapter 2 for a definition and discussion of "Group Consciousness" beings):

> **Group Consciousness Guide**: *A human entity will experience pathways of communication that are unique to their life style, experiences and preferences for communication. For example, one person may get information from a voice in their head, one person may get information from a book that they read, and another may use a deck of cards. Another person may use what we call free writing ... Excuse us ... We are all sorting this out. Group consciousness works a little differently in these kinds of conversations. We are getting lots of information and are trying to organize and distill. Is this making sense to you? Are we being clear?*

> **Howard**: *Yes, you are. Thank you.*

Some highly developed spiritual beings from other civilizations who normally communicate only with other spiritual beings have interestingly expressed a 'learning curve' when communicating with humans for the first time:

> **Howard**: *Can you tell me a bit about your civilization and culture? Is there one race or many races on your home world?*

> **Being**: *We would ask, Howard, that for initial contact, as we are learning to communicate with you, to please ask fairly specific questions. You asked a question about general culture. We will need more guidance. Are you understanding?*

Howard: *Yes.*

Being: *We are looking forward to this interchange and we may be visited by another as we become more familiar with this process. The other, if you agree, is a male; I am female. He prefers at this point to observe. Is that agreeable?*

Howard: *Yes, let's start there. Do you normally communicate verbally or telepathically?*

Being: *Telepathically. That is why this process is somewhat new to us because of time lapse, translation, and looking for a more defined vocabulary.*

Purpose And Objectives

The purpose of this book is to explore and discuss some of the many ways in which telepathically or intuitively derived information may be accessed and expressed in our physical world, and to provide a few examples of such from my own experience; however, it is always up to the reader to determine if the information in this book is relevant to his or her own metaphysical explorations and objectives.

Also, importantly, the purpose of this book is not to teach anyone how to channel spirit beings, or to provide a step-by-step procedure for doing so. The Spiritual Journeys method of teaching a person how to access the Spiritual Area through self-hypnosis can only be ethically taught by a Certified Hypnotherapist who is also a trained Spiritual Journeys Teacher; such Teachers whom I have taught and qualified are identified on my website, www.howardbatie.com, with their permission.

The specific objectives to meet the purposes stated above are three-fold: First, to review a few of the many techniques and processes available that can separately be learned and practiced to attain an expanded state of *conscious* spiritual awareness that I just call my Spiritual Area; Secondly, to discuss the specific processes that I have found useful and effective for safely calling forward any spiritual being – such as a Spirit Guide, an Archangel or Ascended Master – to receive specific information and guidance in a conversational experience; and Thirdly, to share some considerations and procedures that I have found useful for managing and sharing information derived from spiritual sources.

Is Channeling Safe?

Yes, as long as one recognizes and practices the procedures that ensure energetic safety. First, you should understand the energetic procedures for allowing an intuitive or telepathic connection to be made with only beings or sources of information who are spiritually advanced and have no intentions of causing confusion or harm of any kind; Secondly, if one does happen to meet an unfriendly being in an expanded state of consciousness, one should know how to safely and permanently remove them from your presence.

Everything in this universe is one form of energy or another, whether that is an inanimate object (e.g., a pencil, car, or building) or whether it is alive (e.g., a flower, animal, or the human body). Energy can also be manifested as a spiritual, or non-physical, essence such as consciousness, thoughts, or intentions. Energy by itself is neutral; however, depending on how it is used or applied, there is also 'good' energy and 'bad' energy because of its result. Examples of 'good' energy are love, joy and compassion on one hand; on the other hand, the energies of greed, hate and fear are considered 'bad,' with a gradual variation in between these extremes. These variations are separated only by the frequency of the energy expressed, with the 'good' energies being much higher in frequency than the lower frequency of the 'bad' energies. And since lower frequency energies cannot exist in an area of higher frequency energy, all we need to do to ensure that we connect and communicate only with 'good' beings, is to ensure that we are within a 'good' energy field when we begin our connection procedures. When surrounded with Light, there can be no Darkness present.

The necessary and sufficient energetic protection can easily be established around you by beginning your expansion of consciousness preparations with a mantra, prayer, or intention that all the energy in your immediate area only be of the highest frequencies and intentions. For instance, the invocation I use to begin a spiritual communication session is: "Dear Creator, I ask that your love and light surround and protect me always! Thank you, thank you, thank you." And when said out loud and feeling the real meaning of every word within your heart center, more of your own intention and energy is placed into the invocation than if it was only thought silently in the mind. If a field of protective energies is not initially established around yourself, your personal energy field may be left open to the consciousness energy of lower-frequency beings, whom I call the Tricksters, Deceivers and Impostors who inhabit the lower frequency levels of the Spirit Realms. Very effective procedures for identifying and removing all lower-frequency Tricksters and Deceivers are discussed in Appendix B.

After the above invocation has cleared the immediate energy field, it is also good to state out loud why you have created this field of protection around you. If your intention is to establish a conversational connection with a spirit being or to receive intuitive guidance or inspiration, you may wish to immediately follow the above invocation for protection with, for example, "I ask that a clear channel of communication NOW be established between me and the highest levels of love and wisdom, and that all information I receive be only for the greatest good of all concerned! Thank you!" If your intention is to provide a local or remote healing session, you may want to invite the Healing Angels, Archangel Raphael, and/or other spirit beings to attend the healing session for the client. With these protections, you can now safely call forward any spiritual being with whom you wish to speak.

Is Channeling Encouraged?

My own spiritual hypnotherapy practice of more than twenty-two years has taught me that verbal channeling of higher-dimensional sources is not only safe when the practitioner is energetically well-prepared, it is also strongly encouraged by the more advanced beings in the spiritual realms who have shared their information. The spiritual consciousnesses of my own Higher Self and Spirit Guide have gently nurtured this inner nudge within me to temporarily connect to and hold conversations with not only the spiritual part of myself, but also with the spiritual consciousness of other beings as well. For example, at one point, when I asked for Archangel Michael to come forward, I asked him if channeling is beneficial and worthwhile. His response was:

> *Yes! It is absolutely beneficial! It is a way to learn about one's self, and to learn from a spiritual entity about how the process of being a physical human occurs. It is a way to find guidance, and a way to learn about what one's own needs and purpose may be... what will work or not work for that individual. Rather than feeling as if you are alone and trying to work out all of the lessons and tribulations within your life by yourself, you begin to understand that there are*

answers available to you and entities and guides who are more than willing to provide that information, but they simply must be asked. As we are each free will individuals, no information or energy is ever forced upon anyone, but it is always there and available. As humans begin to seek information to find out more about themselves, they will want to reach out with their consciousness to the information that is available. They may search through Third Dimensionality, but they will not understand their own Spiritual Journey until they are able go beyond what is seen and heard by the physical senses. They need to be able to reach outward or step away from just what is physical, so that they are able to access all that is available. And it is ALL available. So, yes, it is good!

Once access is made to the Higher Self and the Fifth Dimensional side of that entity (see Appendix B for a discussion of Dimensions of Consciousness)*, or the energy and information that is available outside of Third Dimension, Karma lessons are no longer a necessity because lessons can be understood and learned without having to physically have "done them". Many of those who are becoming in touch with their Higher Selves and who are learning to channel have already been through many of the lessons of Third Dimensionality, and have understood themselves, which is what those lessons are for, to the point that they are ready to access that information on the other side. As you access your Higher Self, those lessons become less and less needed, and soon it is not necessary to learn those lessons by means of Karma.*

Is Channeling For You?

The 'strong nudge' I received to write this book is a powerful example of the support and encouragement from my spiritual mentors to bring my own experience into the awareness of others who may be deciding what to do with their own curiosity to explore and understand 'the other side'. If the information and examples in this book provide a bit of support or encouragement for your own path, then it has served its purpose. However, the examples I provide reflect only one possible pathway (the one I have chosen) for gaining intuitive insight and direction, and there are 'many paths up the mountain'. I will illustrate a few examples of additional ways I have found other than my own preferred pathway of verbal channeling, but it is up to you to decide their relevance for the pathway you choose. Archangel Michael's statement on this subject is:

> It is good that you are mentioning in your book that there are many different ways for each person to work toward being in contact with their Higher Self and Fifth Dimensional Energy, because there are those who will not mesh well with this type of channeling that you have the Higher Self of your channels do. Rather, they would do well to use tools or to use different types of ways of being in touch. But, each is important because each will enhance that individual's acceptance of the Light and movement forward. So, I encourage you to advise those who are interested, to try more than one way in which they may access their Higher Self for the information that is available.

Variety is the spice of life! I invite you to take what feels right to you in your heart from what follows, and leave the rest for someone else. But for goodness sake, Keep Climbing Your Mountain!

Organization Of The Book

Two reliable procedures for establishing conscious connection with one's own Higher Self, Spirit Guide and other spiritual sources have been previously documented in *"Spiritual Journeys: A Practical Methodology for Accelerated Spiritual Development and Experiential Exploration"* and *"Trans-Scalar Healing: Holistic Healing for Self, Others and Gaia."* *Spiritual Journeys* uses a rapid and very reliable self-hypnotic process to move into your Spiritual Area, and *Trans-Scalar Healing* uses a non-hypnotic process involving only breathwork and guided visualization to accomplish the same objective. However, these two techniques are ones that I have been drawn to from the wide variety of practical techniques available. This book addresses several additional examples of how spiritually-derived information may be obtained and expressed in our 3D world, as well some considerations for sharing that information with others.

Chapter 1 – Spiritual Communication Modalities.
What are some of the safe and reliable ways humans can connect with spiritual sources to gain or exchange information?

Chapter 2 – Spiritual Sources Of Information. What
spiritual beings or sources of information are available to provide the information you seek, and what are their characteristics?

Chapter 3 – Exploring Your Spiritual Area. Once
you connect with your Higher Self and Spirit Guide, how can you apply the information and guidance you receive?

Chapter 4 – Accuracy Of Information. How can we be assured that the spiritual information we receive is accurate and beneficial?

Chapter 5 – My Spiritual Journey. This is an account of my personal metaphysical experience from a Multi-Dimensional perspective.

Epilogue.

Appendix A – The Spiritual Discussion Group. The genesis and composition of our Spiritual Discussion Group, of our Spiritual Research Group, and those Channels who have supported the development of this and my previous books.

Appendix B – Dimensions of Consciousness. Archangel Michael's description of the physical, emotional, mental and spiritual energies that comprise each of the five lower dimensions (levels) of consciousness and physicality on Earth.

Appendix C – Sharing Channeled Information. Suggested considerations for transcribing, archiving and sharing the information received during channeling sessions are provided.

Chapter 1
Communication Modalities

Many spiritual communication techniques have been used with varying degrees of popularity throughout our written human history. In fact, it seems that there are as many different techniques as there are people, and this is proper since there is no single "right" technique for all people. Humans are very creative and tend to invent what works best for them. This chapter summarizes a small portion of techniques or modalities that have allowed humans to obtain varying degrees of information from beyond their physical world and their own knowledge, and to then express that information in their own way.

Some techniques allow for only a limited amount of information to be accessed; for example, there are many questions to which a binary Yes or No answer is appropriate, or questions that might be answered correctly by Yes-Positive-True or No-Negative-False. Alternatively, other techniques provide a more interactive conversational style or situation for transfer of information. In other words, what is "right" for one person might be quite unsatisfactory for another. The proper information pathway for an individual seeking information or guidance will always be the one that is easiest for them to use and provides the desired level of understanding. Many variables will affect this choice, including their language structure, their vocabulary level, their ability and training to comprehend information related to their topic of interest, the degree of information detail needed, and how they plan to use the information requested, to list just a few.

Yes/No Techniques

If only a limited amount of information is sought, use of a pendulum (described below) can, with training, be confidently used to provide an answer to questions such as "Will the baby be a boy or a girl?" or "Should I take this new job opportunity – Yes or No?" or "Is this natural supplement safe or harmful for me?" To be most useful, however, the answer provided will need to come from your Higher Self, not from your conscious mind that might have an investment in one answer or another. Your Higher Self will always provide an answer that is in your own highest and best good, but not necessarily the one you might *consciously* want to hear.

One of the most ancient, and yet easiest to use, devices is a simple pendulum. A pendulum is a small object suspended on a thread or string about six to eight inches long. It can be successfully made of conducting metal, insulators such as plastic or glass, a paper clip, wood of all types, stone beads, brass nuts, or a chip of ceramic tile. They all work equally well, with the main difference being that the heavier pendulums take longer to start moving than the lighter pendulums. Also, the length and weight of the string or line connected to the pendulum will also have an effect on their movement. However, in my experience, a pendulum made of a material that you have a good feeling about will usually give the most pronounced response.

In order to receive consistently reliable results from a pendulum, it must be "programmed" to respond to a specific set of conditions in a certain way. For instance, you can specify that the pendulum's reaction of a "Yes, Positive or True" be a linear, swinging motion toward and away from your body, and a "No, Negative or False" response be a linear, swinging motion perpendicular to that, across your body from right to left. You could just as easily program the pendulum to respond in just the reverse manner, but the essential component that determines how your pendulum will respond is your intention!

A good example of this power of intention can be demonstrated by programming your pendulum to respond to "Yes, Positive or True" toward and away from your body if you are holding the pendulum in front of you, and "No, Negative or False" in a perpendicular direction sideways across your body. To program it in this manner, simply concentrate your vision and mental focus on the pendulum, and say out loud, "Pendulum, I intend that this motion (physically move the pendulum) toward and away from my body represents Yes, Positive or True, and that this motion (again, physically moving the pendulum) across my body represents No, Negative or False." It is just that simple!

To test the pendulum, hold your left hand horizontally in front of you with the palm down and the fingers relaxed but spread far apart. Now, holding the pendulum string in your right hand, brace your right elbow firmly against your side to minimize any unintended motion of the pendulum, and place the body of the pendulum about a half-inch directly in front of the tip of your left index finger. In a moment, it will start to move in the direction that you have programmed for Yes, Positive or True (parallel toward and away from the tip of your finger). Now move the pendulum to about a half-inch from the tip of your middle finger, and it will begin to move in the direction that you have programmed for No, Negative or False. This corresponds to the positive and negative polarities of the energy meridians that extend through these two fingers, a Positive polarity in your Index Finger, and a Negative polarity in your Middle Finger. This "spike" of energy extends several inches beyond the end of your fingertips out into the area beyond the tip of your finger.

Now for the fun part. Reprogram the pendulum in just the reverse fashion to respond to a "Yes, Positive or True" with a horizontal motion back and forth across your body, and a "No, Negative False" with a horizontal motion toward and away from your body, and retest the same index and middle fingers. Miraculously, the *newly programmed response* will now be observed in the pendulum, and will be opposite to the response demonstrated in the first programming! Truly, this is mind over matter, and there is no way to misinterpret what you have just seen.

The intention you stated out loud when programming your pendulum was heard by your Higher Self, which has caused the pendulum to move in the direction you most recently requested. Simply by changing your thought form, you are able to change how you influence the movement of a physical object! However, the amount of information "communicated" from your Higher Self to your physical body and observed with your own eyes is quite limited to one of two possible words: Yes or No, Positive or Negative, False or True. In order to receive more detailed information, instead of just a simple binary Yes or No response, interactive communication techniques that allow use of a greater vocabulary and understanding must be employed.

Interactive Techniques

For those times when you're looking for more detailed information from your inner wisdom, you may want to move beyond the techniques that can provide a simple Yes or No answer to questions you may have. For these times, several modalities and techniques are available that support a more interactive dialog between your conscious thinking mind that asks the questions and the subconscious or spiritual aspect of your being that has the answers and can provide the requested information in a variety of formats. The point here is that there is no single communication technique that is right for everyone, or for that matter, no single "enlightenment modality" that is right for everyone. Explore the options that are available to you and investigate further those that 'feel the best' to you, or that you're drawn to.

Guided Visualization. While I was living in the Virginia Beach, VA area from 1995-1998, I attended nearly a dozen different classes in a wide variety of meditation techniques that supposedly would teach me how to expand my awareness and reach a state of enlightenment and spiritual bliss. Nearly all of them asked me, in some form or another, to quiet my mind and open to the grandeur of the Universe. As an ex-engineer who had spent nearly all my professional lifetime analyzing technical and system-wide engineering challenges for military satellite communications systems, asking me to quiet my mind just didn't work, and I usually ended up analyzing why it wasn't working. Staring at that candle flame or a spot on the wall for several minutes didn't get me any closer to my intended state of Samadhi, or enlightenment, and Buddhist approaches for stilling my analytical, decision-making mind didn't work for me either, although they seemed to work very well for some in the class.

Then I found the Seven Terraces Meditation technique developed by the late Rev. Paul Solomon. Instead of asking me to quiet my mind, this technique provided a guided visualization filled with rich imagery (I'm a very visual person) that kept my conscious mind focused on a fairly fast-paced journey through a meadow, across a stream and up a steep mountainside, and all the way to the top of the snow-covered mountain. In addition, the carefully-crafted imagery provided a metaphorical journey through all the physical senses of my everyday consciousness, across a bridge into my inner spiritual awareness, up through the seven colored terraces of my auric energy system (chakras) and into my Temple Within at the top of the mountain where I could begin to explore my own spiritual abilities.

The analytical, logical type of thinker might do well to learn a bit more about this technique that worked very well for me. Rev. Solomon's Seven Terraces Meditation is featured on the website for the Paul Solomon Foundation, www.paulsolomon.com. Sharon Solomon, Paul's widow, has given me permission to adapt Paul's workshop notes to include the additional spiritual imagery that appeared to me while practicing the Seven Terraces Meditation. With this new experience, I renamed my adaptation as the Inner Light Consciousness (ILC) Meditation, after the Paul's Church of the Inner Light Consciousness that he founded in Virginia Beach. My ILC Meditation and its supporting workbook can be freely downloaded from the ILC Meditation page on my website, www.howardbatie.com, but I'll alert you in advance … as with anything worth working for, there's some homework involved!

Energetic Manipulation. Several energy healing techniques are found by most people to be very relaxing and soothing physically and emotionally. When facilitated by someone you trust and connect with, techniques that involve physical touch are particularly effective for quieting the human Sympathetic Nervous System that supports physical and emotional Fight-or-Flight responses and activities, and instead activates the Parasympathetic Nervous System that promotes both physical and mental relaxation; in addition, increased health and functionality is stimulated at both the cellular and organic levels. A soothing non-therapeutic Swedish Massage, especially when provided by a practitioner who is also trained in a relaxing energy healing technique, is very relaxing to both body and mind. Both the client and the practitioner often feel a much deeper, relaxing connection as their mind's normal busy brain-wave activity gently gives way to the slower, more calming feelings and sensations felt in the slower brain-wave states where both healing and opening to a higher level of awareness can begin to occur. A detailed discussion of the Human Energy Field (HEF) and how specific energy healing techniques can positively affect the HEF for increased health and wellness can be found in my 2003 book, *"Healing Body, Mind & Spirit: A Guide To Energy Based Healing."*

Reiki. Reiki (pronounced **RAY**-kee) is a Japanese word for Divine Light (Rei) and Universal Life Force (Ki), and is a system of natural healing that channels a specific frequency of spiritual healing energy through the practitioner's hands. Reiki is said to accesses the source of Life itself, and can be a catalytic factor to heal one's self, and others as well, on the mental, emotional and physical levels. Reiki allows the source of well-being to enhance and balance natural life forces through non-intrusive therapeutic touch. Health maintenance, pain relief, mental quietude and healing can result from its application. Reiki augments and accelerates the client's own healing process, and can be effective when the client does not respond to other forms of treatment.

Reiki is not a system of religious beliefs; the world does not need another. Reiki is taught by a Teacher, called a Reiki Master, to his or her students in a series of energetic 'attunements' that have the effect of providing significantly higher frequency energies to the student's chakras and energy field, or aura. The student can then, in turn, provide this healing energy to others. Anyone can learn the fundamentals of Reiki and become a very effective healer for "laying on of hands". However, dedication and practice are necessary to become proficient in the use of that energy and to understand the principles of how to direct this healing energy for the highest good of yourself and of your clients.

After several years' experience providing Reiki sessions to my clients, and seeing and hearing of the wonderful results it provided for them, I asked a Channel I trusted (the late Carla Reuckert, co-author of *The Law Of One* and author of *A Channeling Handbook*) for additional information about how this particular healing energy could affect the human body and its energetic aura. The following response was provided by Q'uo, the Group Consciousness Entity channeled in 2006 by Ms. Reuckert:

> **Howard**: *"As a practicing Reiki Master-Teacher, I'm interested in what Q'uo has to offer about Reiki energy. Specifically, I'd like to know what can be shared about the nature of the physical and spiritual characteristics of this energy that, in my experience, can bring about profound improvements. What are the mechanisms by which Reiki energy can heal? How are the physical cells in the body affected by Reiki energy? Is it necessary for the recipient to believe in and accept Reiki energy for healing to occur? What is the source of Reiki energy? Is Reiki energy protected or guided by higher spiritual beings?"*

> **Carla:** *We are those of the Q'uo, and are aware of your query. We are not aware, because this instrument (Carla) is not aware, of the roots of the meaning of Reiki. We do not know this word as such. However, we examine the physical vehicle of this instrument which has experienced a great deal of Reiki energy given through various practitioners and Masters of that art. We would say that this energy is the energy of the One Infinite Creator which is modified by its travel through the chakra system or the electrical body of the practitioner who is offering healing. It is not at all an energy which comes from*

the practitioner. Your entire (physical and energetic) body may be easily tuned and magnetized to whatever vibration you wish to tune it. This instrument also carefully tunes its physical body, as well as its energy body, before each session of channeling by singing hymns, offering prayers, and so forth.

In the Reiki energy exchange, Infinite Love comes into the physical and electrical body system of the practitioner of Reiki. That practitioner breaks itself open, blesses its unique vibrational characteristics, and offers them to the energy that is coming through. The energy that is coming through is then blessed by the Reiki Master, who releases it in its altered form to flow into the energy system of the patient. Thereby, an impersonal, universal energy has been particularized and personalized by the genuine love and the open-hearted compassion of the practitioner. This is not done in any kind of intellectual way. In fact, when intellect is applied to this art, it falls apart. It must be done from direct feeling – that is the way the heart thinks. The heart knows, and then immediately it produces that which, in thinking, would be a process.

The energies of Reiki move through each cell, and their information is coded so that each cell may pick up the energy involved. Let us be clear in stating that there is no push or pull to Reiki energy. It is not something that is given. It is, rather, an environment that is created. For the time that the Reiki work is being done, the client lies in an increasing Edenic environment. The distortions that create illness are suspended. The nature of the energy pouring through creates an alternative environment, and if the person chooses to accept the new environment, healing may occur. If the person chooses not to accept the new healing environment, then it is as if it never occurred. No harm has been done, but also no healing will have occurred.

It is not at all necessary for an entity who is being healed to believe that anything is occurring; however, it IS necessary for the entity to accept the new configuration of energy. It is not belief that is necessary, but a willingness to accept a new environment is required.

Additional information about Reiki, as well as for locating a trained Reiki Teacher, can be found at www.reiki.org.

Healing Touch. The Healing Touch Program is another direct energetic manipulation technique that teaches the practitioner how to use the elements of their own energy field (Chakras, Acupuncture Meridians, and Energy Bodies) to beneficially affect the energy field of their client, who is normally lying on a portable massage table or healing table in the practitioner's physical presence. Energy affects energy, and through a learned set of specific hand motions through the client's surrounding energy field (aura), the energies in and around the practitioner's hands can affect the energy flow in the client's energy field to stimulate the immune system, accelerate the repair of damaged tissue and significantly reduce physical pain, all of which also promote stimulation of the Parasympathetic Nervous System and its relaxing and self-healing abilities.

The Healing Touch Program was developed by the late Janet Mentgen, RN, a clairvoyant who could visually see the human energetic aura; through her medical training as a Registered Nurse, she was able to observe and correlate the changes in a patient's energetic aura when specific hand motions were used on or above the patient. Healing Touch was developed for use primarily by other nurses and caregivers; however, any person can be trained to provide the energetic benefits of Healing Touch. The Healing Touch Program is also a complete credentialing program to train Certified Healing Touch Practitioners, and is one of the most-recognized energy healing techniques now being incorporated into the services of many progressive hospitals around the world. Additional information about Healing Touch and its training program can be found at www.healingtouchprogram.com.

Ro-Hun Transformational Therapy. Ro-Hun incorporates both energetic manipulation and hypnotherapeutic regression processes, and is designed to release all the major negative issues that may have resulted from previous emotionally traumatic situations, regardless of whether they were experienced during childhood, while unborn and still in the womb, or in a prior lifetime. As the energy patterns around a chakra that is operating sub-optimally are 'stirred up' by the Practitioner's moving hands, the information in negative energy patterns are brought up to the conscious mind and described as a current lifetime, in-womb or Past life Regression viscerally experienced by the client. When the client consciously understands how the negative energy in that prior experience is affecting his or her life today, they are guided by the Ro-Hun Therapist to permanently release the negative energy and its influence, and to replace it with positive energy patterns that empower the client's understanding of the issue, as well as their self-confidence and inner strength. This process is repeated several times in each major chakra until all the significant or limiting "Faulty Thoughts" are completely removed from the client's mental and emotional energy bodies. Examples of a Faulty Thoughts include: I am unworthy of love,

I am afraid of making a mistake, I must judge others to protect myself, there is never enough, etc.

An example of how this communication proceeds from the client's Higher Self to the practitioner is illustrated below and is also provided as one of the actual case studies provided in my earlier book, "*Healing Body, Mind & Spirit.*" Jane (not her real name) had come to me for a series of Ro-Hun sessions to release several emotional issues that had been bothering her. During the initial interview, she said that among the many issues she wanted to address was her relationship with her teenage son; he seemed to do everything possible to annoy, irritate, and anger Jane, with no apparent reason to her.

After coaching Jane into a state of very deep physical and mental relaxation, I was loosening and stirring up the energy patterns in the emotional energies above her Solar Plexus chakra, the center of her own personal power over her own life, as well as over others. When I asked Jane what she was feeling and what she was aware of, she reported verbally that she "saw" a large, heavy box on her chest and "felt" it pressing down terribly hard, crushing the breath out of her. From her wincing grimace and labored breath on the healing table, she was obviously vividly experiencing these feelings in her mind. However, I recognized that the box was only a symbol representing something else in her subconscious mind. When I asked her to let the pain go away and to look inside the box, she reported that she saw "two round things" in there. I asked her to take the first round thing out and look at in the light so she could see what it really was. As she did so, she said it was a large, metallic wood screw about two inches long, but all of a sudden she felt it buried in her neck and she was bleeding severely. She also felt the pain in the side of her neck very clearly, so I again suggested that the pain would go away and the bleeding stop for now, but all other details would remain very clear so we could understand them. She felt that she was dying and was very confused, upset and angry.

Then I calmed her and asked her to look at the box on her chest again, and take out the second round thing so we could see what it was. As she brought the round thing out into the light, she said it became a small statue of a horse-drawn chariot. I then asked her to move her awareness into the chariot, feel herself holding the reins of the chariot, and to look around and tell me what she was seeing. Almost immediately, she started describing a chariot race in which she was a man about 22 years old racing with seven other charioteers in a large, oval open-air amphitheater. She described in detail the smell of the dust and the sound of the horses' hooves as they raced around the course. In her mind, she was experiencing this race first-hand, and to her subconscious mind it did not matter whether it was one of her previous lives in which she incarnated as a man, or whether she connected with a remote event in someone else's life. For some reason, her subconscious mind had connected with this particular experience from the past and was now replaying it for her. And she was actually reliving that experience now on the table in the sense that she was able to describe the smells, hear the sounds and see the events as clearly as if she were really there in person.

As she/he rounded the pylon at one end of the race course, he saw he was swiftly coming up on the chariot of his friend, and he planned to sideswipe his friend, cause him to crash and then he could go on to win the race. As we examined this plan, Jane came to understand that her/his Faulty Thought was "I can control others to get what I want." But as he rammed his own chariot into that of his friend, his own wheel cracked instead, and he was thrown from his chariot, which then fell on top of him, crushing his chest. The chariot was, of course, the large heavy box which Jane had felt was crushing her chest. Also, as the chariot fell, a large metal screw was loosened and was rammed into his neck and tore it open. As he lay dying under his chariot, his last thoughts were, "I'm better than this! This isn't supposed to be happening!" I then asked Jane what she would like to do about this scene, and she immediately said, "I need to change what happened." So, I asked her to move back into the race just before he ran into his friend, and asked him how he would like to change the events if he could. He responded, "Don't run into my friend!" So, I then asked him to watch the race as an observer as they both raced side by side toward the finish line. However, neither he nor his friend won the race, so sideswiping his friend would have been in vain anyway.

After the race, I was intuitively guided to ask the young charioteer and his friend to embrace in friendship as gallant competitors and go to the local tavern to celebrate with a little ale. While they were laughing and talking with each other, I was again guided to ask the young man to look deep into the eyes of his friend, and I asked Jane if she recognized this friend. She shouted, "Oh, My God! It's my son!" The next day Jane called to say that there had been a remarkable turnaround in the attitude of her son toward her, and that he had actually sat down with her and discussed how he felt about himself with her! When the negative beliefs and thought patterns in her own energy field were removed, the way that her energy field interacted with her son's energy field had changed significantly!

This case study was purposefully selected to illustrate two very important facets of Ro-Hun Transformational Therapy: First, although the initial energetic coaching into a state of deep physical and mental relaxation was not a hypnotic induction as such, it achieved the same objective of hypnosis in that a vivid Past Life Regression experience resulted; and Second, successful reframing, releasing and complete removal of the emotional mental issue or Faulty Thought depends heavily on the practitioner's training and presence in dealing with highly charge emotional experiences while in an altered state of awareness. Such training is provided in the Ro-Hun training program, and proficiency in its application must be demonstrated before the practitioner can be Certified as a Ro-Hun Therapist.

Not coincidentally, this case study illustrates that the whole key to the past life experience was initially presented to Jane's conscious mind in the form of symbols – the box on her chest and the "two round things" in it that needed to be explored and understood further. Both the Ro-Hun and Hypnotherapy training programs heavily stress the importance of examining any symbols that are presented. For more information on how you can become a Ro-Hun Therapist, or to locate a trained Ro-Hun Transformational Therapist for your own self-healing journey, see Delphi University's website at www.delphiu.com.

Automatic Writing. Automatic Writing can best be described as opening one's awareness and allowing one's own Higher Self (or another non-physical being under the approval and guidance of the Higher Self) to temporarily assume control of the motor functions of the hands and arms that are normally used for writing in longhand or typing on a keyboard.

Longhand. Transcription of spiritual or intuitively-derived information through longhand writing was practiced before the advent of typewriters; later, computers significantly speeded up the information recording process. The Channel gets into a comfortable seated or reclining position and, while holding a pen or pencil and paper to write on, uses their own relaxation technique or process to expand their awareness into what I call their Spiritual Area, connects with their own Higher Self, and allows themselves to become a passive instrument (not an analyzer) of whatever their hand would begin to write on the paper. Usually, it will be written words in the language of the individual, or it might be a graphic picture or image with the message's information encoded in its design, such as described below in the information about Entura Art.

Normally, a significant amount of practice is required to record complex thoughts and concepts as written words, because the Channel must learn to suspend all judgement or even thinking about what is being written or drawn. With sufficient practice, the writing becomes clearer and the words easier to understand after returning to full conscious awareness. Although somewhat time-consuming, great amounts of information have been provided to those who regularly practice this skill. For example, the entire Ro-Hun Transformational Healing process was initially written in longhand by Patricia Hayes, co-founder of Delphi University, a wonderful metaphysical teaching institution in a beautiful retreat setting near McCaysville, GA.

Computer. A similar process is used here, except that if the Channel is an accomplished touch-typist, the information provided by the spiritual source can be typed and recorded much faster. Suzanne Lie (www.multidimensions.com) and Suzy Ward (www.matthewbooks.com) are two examples of reputable channels who document their conversations with higher dimensional sources by typing on the computer the words they hear intuitively and then sharing them with the public on the Internet. If you are willing to diligently practice automatic writing while at your computer, you may amaze yourself at the positive results and wealth of information that is available for you!

Entura Art. Entura Art is the form of channeled spiritual art developed and advanced by Patricia Hayes, co-founder of Delphi University in northern Georgia. According to Patricia, "Entura" means entering the energy field of a person, object, situation or concept, and is the process of also entering a higher state of consciousness to attune one's self to the energies of the subject and allow the spiritual energies and information to flow to the canvas. Patricia describes her process as sitting with her chalk or pastels and paper, closing her eyes and attuning with her subject while allowing herself to become an empty vessel for the intuitive energies which she attunes to, allowing them to dance across her paper, revealing their message. She then studies and interprets the drawing, its colors and shapes and shades that represents the intuitive understanding and messages related to that subject and to bring about needed and appropriate emotional and spiritual healing. All the various colors and movements of energy have meaning and help us understand a person's past, present and future.

Entura Art uses unique and specific methods of lifting one's awareness into a higher state of consciousness, and then entering the auric/energy field of his/her subject - one's self, another person, a place or thing, a past or present time period, or a spiritual concept like love, harmony, or wisdom. This psychic and spiritual art is a unique method of tuning into energy and translating that energy into color and motion. The Entura Artist becomes a vehicle for spiritual communication, healing, and growth through non-verbal as well as verbal expression. Heightened awareness, spiritual vision and higher perception are awakened in both the artist and the viewer. See www,delphiu.com for further information about Entura Art.

Prayer. Prayer is included here as a modality of communication with higher dimensional beings because nearly every culture and civilization in the world uses one form of prayer or another, depending on their culture, civilization, religion, philosophy or belief system. Prayer is defined by Webster's New World Dictionary as "an address or petition to God or gods in word or thought" for a specified purpose or objective, a plea to a higher power for something that we ask

17

for. Yet in most cases, a prayer is only half of a spiritual conversation in which we ask God, or Allah or whatever higher power we are praying to, for something; the other half is receiving an acknowledgement or response from the higher dimensional source. We are taught in many religious practices to "Ask and ye shall receive," but sometimes keep wondering why it seems that our prayers are not answered.

The simple answer is that we are not usually taught how to recognize the response, which could be in any number of formats other than audibly; but to compound the frustration, we are not taught "the fine print," the conditions under which what we ask for will be granted or provided. However, our Spiritual Research Group has been informed that the spiritual dimensions will always provide an answer to our prayers IF: (1) we are ready to receive and understand the information or gift we are asking for, (2) receiving what we ask for will be in the highest and best good of our physical self and our Higher Self, and (3) receiving what we ask for will cause no harm to any living being, including ourselves. The answer or response may be provided at any time now or in the future, and it may come in an unexpected form, such as "a blessing in disguise."

Communicating With Angels. One of the easiest (and most fun!) methods for communicating with your Guardian Angel is to ask it for what you want, or for what you want them to do. This is a bit like praying in that initially you might only think you are talking TO your Angels, without hearing them audibly answering your requests. Their part of the conversation (the response) is provided in the reliable presentation or manifestation of what you asked for, assuming that the three conditions discussed above have been met. This process has now been elevated to quite an interesting art form described in Tom Moore's book, *"The Gentle Way,"* where he informs us that the proper way to ask for what you want is to ask out loud for the "Most Benevolent Outcome," or MBO, that would occur if your wishes were granted.

So, I tried it out, and said out loud, "Angels I ask for a Most Benevolent Outcome for a parking space right in front of the (hardware store, grocery store or whatever). Thank you!" Always say Thank You. After trying several times for a similar parking space at other stores, I learned that if I give the Angels at least five minutes advance notice, usually an empty parking space will be right there just waiting for me, or as I drive up, someone is just leaving their parking space right in front of the store. Coincidence, right? Well, not when it keeps happening repeatedly! I use it for all occasions, such as, "Angels, I ask for a pleasant and safe trip to Portland Airport and return home. Thank you!" By saying "Thank You" after each request, you are stating to the universe that you know that your request has already been heard and fulfilled, and you are just thanking them for their part of the "conversation."

Requesting a Most Benevolent Outcome gives the Angelic Kingdom the most opportunity to provide you the absolute best response to your prayer. For example, in a healing situation if the Angels are asked to provide "Complete relief from the Arthritis in Sally's knee," the pain relief for her knee may well be provided, but the Angels would not be allowed to address a greater need for repairing the damaged cartilage that is causing the pain in her knee, because that was not explicitly asked for, and the Angels will not ever override your free will and 'guess' at what you want. A wiser request would be, "Angels, I request a Most Benevolent Outcome for the greatest health and wellness that is in Sally's highest and best good at this time. Thank you." That would address much more than just her knee.

If you're asking for something for someone else instead of for yourself, Mr. Moore suggests that you modify the request slightly into a "Benevolent Prayer," or BP, by saying out loud, "Angels, I request a Benevolent Prayer that Aunt Mary has (a happy and pain-free day, or whatever). Thank you!" Again, you're stating your intention and desire that Aunt Mary has an enjoyable day, and then giving your prayer over to the Angels to fulfill, if the three prior conditions have been met. More information and examples of how to begin this powerful two-way "dialog" with your Angels can be found at www.thegentleway.com.

Verbal Channeling. The several methods of verbally channeling discussed here can be organized into two main styles: Self-Directed Channeling and Externally Directed Channeling. In Self-Directed Channeling, there needs to be only two participants: the human Channel and the non-physical Source of the information being provided. The Channel enters a state of expanded awareness and invites a spiritual being with whom they have an energetic agreement to speak through the voice of the Channel and deliver a message on the topic usually chosen by the Channel. Usually there is little, if any, conversational exchange between the Channel and the Source.

In Externally Directed Channeling, however, there are three participants: the Channel who places themselves into a greatly expanded state of conscious awareness, the spiritual Source of the information being provided, and an external Director who remains fully conscious and enters a conversational dialog with the spiritual Source of the information. This could be the Higher Self or Guide of the Channel, or another spiritual being altogether, such as an Archangel or Ascended Master. This approach allows for immediate clarification or addition of details if the intended meaning of the spiritual Source's information is not clearly understood.

The following description of each style provides only a few examples of the many individual methods currently available. No attempt is made to rate the relative quality or validity of each style, or of the individual methods within each style.

Self-Directed Channeling. This style of communication involves only the person who is channeling and the source of information, which can be quite varied, as illustrated by the following examples from just a very small sampling of those available on the Internet.

Suzanne Ward channels her son Matthew who died in 1980. Matthew chose as a pre-incarnation soul contract to physically die at the young age of 17, and in 1994 began sending telepathic messages to his mother regarding current Earth political, institutional, economic and other public events and issues so that the information could be published in books for the public. She makes daily contact with her son in "Nirvana" and types the telepathically received messages and information on her computer; she then publishes a monthly Internet digest of relevant current events as viewed from "the other side", as well as compilations of several sessions in book form. The messages from Matthew are posted on her website (www.matthewbooks.com), and voice synthesized audio versions of her transcribed channeling sessions are available at www.youtube.com (search for matthewbooks).

Steve Rother channels a Group Consciousness Entity that calls itself simply "The Group". His channeling segment is introduced by his partner Barbara who initially sets the ambiance with a short breathing and light meditation, but she does not otherwise influence the channeling or direct interactive questions to The Group during the channeling. Steve provides a televised monthly video production of his

21

channeling sessions; once in an expanded state of conscious awareness, he usually remains seated and appears fully conscious with his eyes open to the point where he can direct a computer mouse to highlight an illustration of the information he is channeling. Steve's videos are available for viewing at www.youtube.com (search for "Steve Rother").

Darryl Anka channels a multidimensional being from the future called Bashar, who provides a wide-ranging discussion on many topics with humor, insight, and quite animated gesturing to emphasize his points. Mr. Anka channels both seated with his eyes closed and standing, and he occasionally accepts questions for Bashar from guests in his audience. His website is www.bashar.org, and his videos are also available at www.youtube.com (search for Darryl Anka).

Ronna Herman Vezane has provided, for several years, a monthly message from Archangel Michael on many spiritual topics including where we are collectively in the current spiritual ascension process, observations pertaining to our struggles with the polarity and division with our political, philosophical, economic and religious institutions, and much more. These transcribed channelings are posted on her website www.ronnastar.com, and she also conducts widely-attended workshops on personal and spiritual development and expansion. Her many channeling and training workshop videos are available on www.youtube.com (search for Ronna Herman Vezane).

Natalie Glasson (www.omna.org) offers teaching workshops, personalized healing services and channelings from a wide variety of sources including Archangels, Ascended Masters, Elemental Earth Energies, and other spiritual beings; channelings are available in audible format, written transcriptions, and video presentations, both on her website and on www.youtube.com (search for Natalie Glasson).

Trans-Scalar Healing (TSH) is a recent form of self-directed channeling that has been developed for the purpose of providing remote spiritual healing energies to a person or situation anywhere in the world. The TSH practitioner moves their awareness into their Spiritual Area without the use of self-hypnotic techniques and instead uses a focused, intentional breathing process to expand their awareness into their Spiritual Area where they communicate directly with the Higher Self of their client, who is normally not in the physical presence of the practitioner. Additionally, direct telepathic communication is established with the group of healing Angels who are called by the client's Higher Self to come and only *assist* the practitioner as he or she provides higher-dimensional Scalar healing energies, or the energies of other healing techniques they are trained in (e.g., Reiki, Healing Touch, etc.). As the healing sequence progresses, the Angels support the practitioner by confirming or amending the telepathic information received by the practitioner; the practitioner opens their eyes to write down the information received from the Angels, and then returns to the healing process without breaking their state of expanded awareness. This entire process can be taught to anyone who is interested in learning remote healing techniques, and is documented in detail in my 2017 book, *"Trans-Scalar Healing: Holistic Healing for Self, Earth and Gaia."*

Externally Directed Channeling. An externally directed channeling session is composed of three participants: the Channel, who places themselves in an expanded state of awareness and openness to the energies of higher dimensional beings; the Director, who remains fully conscious and asks the questions to be answered; and the spiritual Source of the information being brought forward through the Channel and spoken to the Director. In addition, the Source may simultaneously include more than one individual spiritual entity such as Ascended Masters, Archangels, Spirit Guides, the Akashic Records, etc.

Local Psychic Readings. Intuitive or Psychic Readings may be performed by an adept psychic either locally where the recipient of the information is in the physical presence of the psychic, or remotely where the psychic provides the information to the client by telephone, written transcript or other means of communication. In a locally conducted channeling session, the psychic would often ensure that a positive energetic connection is made between themselves and their client, either by expanding their aura to surround the client or by physically touching the client, such as holding their hands. The psychic would then open their awareness to the energies in the client's aura, which contains the vibrational patterns of the client's entire soul experiences, and report what they become aware of. In this case, the psychic acts as the Director, and the client's Higher Self acts as the Source of the information that is transferred energetically or intuitively to the Director and relayed verbally, or by some other means, to the client's conscious mind.

Remote Psychic Sessions. In a remotely conducted channeling session, the procedure is essentially the same as a Local Psychic Reading, except that the psychic makes their energetic connection with the client on the intuitive or energetic level instead of on the physical level. Usually, all that is required is that the psychic have some personal information about the client, such as their name, age and physical location at the agreed date and time for the psychic to conduct the session. This allows the psychic to "tune into" the energies of the client wherever they are and become aware of the client's energies/information. Interestingly, it is not necessary for the adept psychic to know in advance the reason for conducting the session or the client's situation about which additional information has been requested. Adept psychics who conduct remote sessions to investigate a client's physical or emotional conditions are sometimes called Medical Intuitives, and often provide their services as a potential source of additional information for further consideration at the request of a licensed medical practitioner.

Spiritual Research Group. The Spiritual Research Group that has supported the development of this book, as well as my others, consists of over a dozen students who have been trained in a simple and effective self-hypnotic technique to very quickly expand their awareness and enter their Spiritual Area. These techniques are necessarily taught by a Certified Hypnotherapist and are described in my book, "*Spiritual Journeys: A Practical Methodology for Accelerated Spiritual Development and Experiential Exploration.*" It takes only just a few seconds for the Channel to become ready to support a fully interactive conversation between the conscious Director and the spiritual (non-physical) Source, which may simultaneously consist of, for example, the Channel's Higher Self and Spirit Guide, the Director's Higher Self and Spirit Guide, one or more Ascended Masters, an Archangel and/or additional higher dimensional spiritual entities, depending on who is called forward to 'speak'. The Director remains fully conscious and aware to ask specific questions, guide the two-way conversation between themselves and the Source of the information, and to request clarification when needed. A convenient and workable protocol has been established to ensure that all spiritual participants have an opportunity to provide information, but always only one at a time to identify the entity 'speaking' through the Channel.

Chapter 2

Spiritual Sources Of Information

In practicing The Art Of Metaphysical Communication, it is important to understand with whom we are communicating. Just as there are several levels of understanding and knowledge among the people with whom we physically interact on a daily basis, there are also several levels of experience and wisdom among the spiritual beings in the unseen worlds beyond our physical senses. With the verbal channeling method provided by the Spiritual Journeys process, we have been provided with reliable methods that allow us to conversationally communicate with many higher beings from whom we can learn a great deal about who and what we truly are and how the spiritual or non-physical realms operate. One of the first things we learned when we began to communicate directly with non-physical beings is that the way that humans think and act in our physical environment is markedly different from the way most non-physical beings think and act in their metaphysical realms of consciousness. These opposite philosophical concepts were introduced in *The Law Of One* as the Service To Self (STS) and the Service To Others (STO) camps, and are summarized below and discussed further in Appendix B.

The Law Of One
In their seminal five-volume treatise called *"The Ra Material: The Law Of One,"* Elkins, McCarty and Reuckert identified the root cause of all conflict and discord in our 3D physical and 4D astral worlds to be the two opposing philosophies for conscious beings to attain a higher degree of spiritual enlightenment. A being may follow either the principles and precepts of Service To Self (Duality/Polarity/Competition) or of Service To Others (Unity, Cooperation and Oneness with all Life) as a valid

pathway to higher enlightenment. Service To Self followers believe that personal and individual safety and security belong only to those who rule over others who are weaker; therefore, 'goodness' is defined by strength and cunning. Conversely, Service To Others followers believe that every conscious being is connected to and is a manifested spark of Creator, with no one individual being better or worse, above or below another.

From a metaphysical perspective, both pathways are equally valid up to a point. We have all been given Free Will to choose whatever we want without fear of being judged harshly by an external God "up there" for exercising our Free Will and to choose either pathway. However, that may not really be apparent to proponents of either 'side' until they both evolve to the higher consciousness level called Fifth Dimension of Consciousness, 5D (see Appendix B). At that point, 5D STS beings cannot evolve further, since they always see the wisdom of altering their belief patterns to those of the STO camp, and the unity consciousness of the STO path prevails in the remainder of the spiritual evolution pathway for all souls. Beginning in 5D, and in all levels of evolution above 5D, competition is replaced by cooperation, and all actions, thoughts and deeds are made according to what is in the highest and best good of all concerned (unity consciousness) instead of domination and power over others (what's in it for me) of the STS followers. Thought and information transfer begins to be done telepathically instead of verbally in 5D, and because we will all eventually become telepathic, we will also be aware of the sender's thoughts, feelings and motives in addition to the information they provide. Therefore, there is no need or even desire for deception, lies or untruths in the information exchange at that level and above.

The point is that, until we evolve to 5D or above, we must be careful to choose with whom we establish conscious spiritual communication. So, let's look at the range of spiritual beings who are present in the Astral (4D) and Spiritual (5D and above) Realms we now have access to.

Conscious Spiritual Beings

In order to understand the way the non-physical reality 'works,' we first must release the need to think of any hierarchy of spiritual beings, such as thinking or believing, for instance, that an Archangel is "higher" or "better" than an Angel. They simply have different functions, but the signature vibration of an Archangel may be higher or lower *in frequency of vibration* than that of another individual spiritual consciousness, depending on their respective ranges of experience and consequent stages of spiritual evolution or 'ascension'. The higher a spiritual being vibrates, the more energetic it becomes and the stronger their energy field is; therefore, the highest possible vibrational energy is that of Creator. Creator's creations are always somewhat less energetic than Its own, resonating with the same purpose, but of lower frequency.

The Elohim. The Elohim are a collective group of individual spiritual beings (the singular is Eloha) who are energetically very close to the energy of The Creator Of All That Is. Our Spiritual Research Group is particularly fortunate to include a Channel whose Higher Self is associated with the Elohim; this provides a unique opportunity to understand the role and functions of the Elohim from this first-hand perspective and experience, as translated by that Channel's Higher Self:

The Elohim are the first creation of The Creator as a method by which Creation could be disseminated in a variety of pathways and at a variety of levels. The Elohim were born directly of The Creator and given consciousness to allow them their function, but they are without ego, without division. The Elohim are responsible for the direct creation of the souls and life forms, following the directive of The Creator, as well as for gathering information to help make it so. For example, their emissaries and messengers to Earth discovered what was necessary to create positive life for Earth in that environment, and when all was good, they were allowed by Creator to manifest life on the Earth.

The Elohim are also the creators of the human soul essence that incarnates into a physical body on Earth, and their work is deeply sacred. To serve in the Angelic Kingdom as an Eloha depicts great honor and trust. Each of their Angelic functions is sacred. It cannot go wrong, and it cannot be misused, but Elohim and all Angelic Kingdom beings have awareness of a special trust and a deep gift from the Creator.

It is nearly impossible to describe Creator, and it is impossible for you to understand the full significance, the full experience of the creative energy of Source. We only ask that as you attempt to do that, you keep in mind that we are not talking about a specific being, but a force, an energy consciousness which knows no limitations, no boundaries, and operates from a set of rules of its own. If Source intends to create a specific item, such as a soul, a planet or a galaxy, that intention and creative energy comes to us, the Elohim, both as a group consciousness and to some degree individually, depending on the need for our specific strengths and talents. We Elohim individually have preferences for the type of energy projects we assist with, and our individual talents are connected to, and eventually blended with, each other in a group project and consciousness. It is as if each of us were an individual member in an orchestra, but when combined together we then create a fuller, stronger "musical" representation. The larger the project (for instance, a galaxy instead of an individual soul), the more "orchestra" members or Elohim that are needed. Depending on the theme, the project to be created, it can be as few as ten or twelve Elohim, and as many as several hundred.

Source's mechanism of deciding what is needed is not as well-defined as your process of deciding; it is an impulse, it is a "happening," and it is what needs to happen next. When this creative urge, this energy and intention, comes forth from Creator, the Elohim are the first recipient of that information, and the impulse comes almost simultaneously to both the Elohim and the Archangels. Archangels are slightly more well-defined than the Elohim, but the difference is at times insignificant; however, we receive these impulses and intuitively understand what is to be the final project, and we begin to pull together what is needed for its initial shaping and existence. The messengers that we send out find and call together what is needed, such as additional information of a specific nature for the final part of that process. Then as the project objectives become more well-defined, the "skeleton and the flesh" as you would say, are defined and brought into existence, but a galaxy is a very different consciousness with a very different set of operating procedures than, for example, a human or even a planet.

We do not mean to confuse you, Howard; it is only that occasionally you wander into topics which we love to share and explore, but are a challenge to bring down to your level of understanding without diminishing the opportunity for you to somehow grasp what is behind what we are explaining.

Archangels And Angels. The class of spiritual beings we call Archangels (from the Greek, 'Arch' meaning 'chief' or 'highest') are mentioned by name in all the Abrahamic religions (Islam, Christianity, Judaism), as well as Eastern Orthodox, Zoroastrianism, and others; Archangels Michael, Raphael, and Gabriel are the three most often mentioned. However, our Spiritual Research Group has provided the following additional information:

Archangels are closer to Creator, but not quite as close as the Elohim. An Archangel's duties are in the higher realms of the spiritual world where they do most of their work, whereas Angels do most of their work with incarnated beings. I see Archangels moving a lot throughout the spirit world, moving as if they're supervising and checking and monitoring and helping to keep things connected and running smoothly. Archangels move about in the spirit world and work with the Guides a lot. They help with souls who are in between physical lessons, in between incarnations where they've had to learn lessons and they're in the spirit world where they process what they've learned or need to learn.

As the Elohim created life in other beings and on other worlds, the Archangels formed in concert with that world or being. There is an Archangel for each world, for each life form. The Archangel group is an energy of guidance and communication and serves as needed, and for the life of the form or world. There are multitudes of Archangels, thousands, mostly unnamed, some named, with many Archangels currently assigned to Gaia because of the complexity of the life forms and the current evolutionary ascension process. The unnamed Archangels are the worker-bees of the Angelic Kingdom, of the Archangelic form.

The named Archangels with well-defined functions include Archangel Michael (strength and protection), Archangel Raphael (healing), and Archangel Gabriel (discovery and communication). In addition, Archangel Metatron functions as to what is needed at the time to problem-solve. It may be communication, it may be decision-making help, it may be teaching, but he is one who deals more directly with issues.

Only the Elohim are creators of individual souls; however, the Elohim will at times delegate the creative process to a group of Archangels for creation of a physical world, a galaxy, or a universe; however, the Elohim will still oversee that process. The Archangels can and often also work in other universes when Creator requires.

Spiritual Guides & Mentors. A Spirit Guide is a highly evolved member of the spiritual or angelic realms who is assigned to oversee and guide the spiritual development and evolution of each individual soul essence (human and otherwise) upon their creation by Creator. Each Guide is usually responsible for mentoring a small group of from two or three to a dozen or more souls who have the same or similar interests and purposes, for instance, exploration and discovery, healing, musical ability, creativity, etc. Guides do not fully incarnate themselves, and they do confer with one or more Archangels when required. The primary mission of the Guide for each 'pod' of like souls is to advise each individual soul how best stay 'on track' with learning the lessons they have chosen to learn during a physical incarnation. After that lifetime is completed, they assist in the review and evaluation of whether or not the desired objectives for that lifetime were attained and to begin planning for the next physical lifetime.

When asked to comment further on how her own Guide helps to mentor herself, one Channel's Higher Self replied:

> *Every incarnated soul has a spiritual mentor or guide to guide them through the planning and support for each physical incarnation chosen by the soul essence or Higher Self. The Guides are very wise mentors, but sometimes they also need additional advice, and helpful advice is always available from an Archangel. Sometimes a Guide is responsible for as many as twenty or thirty souls, but there can be fifteen or there can be three. When I was created, I was with seven other souls, and we were all a part of our Guide's pod that we called our Soul Group. Our Guide always advises us and helps us to think of new ways, better ways to do something or solving something. If one of us is trying to understand, and our Guide needs additional help, maybe ideas of new ways to help, that's what an Archangel can help with, because they know all.*

Ascended Masters. An Ascended Master is a category of spiritual being who has normally incarnated as a physical human or other Third Dimensional sentient lifeform on Earth or on another physical world, has learned all the lessons necessary for them to learn in this dimension of consciousness, and has returned to the spiritual world without the need to reincarnate again. They also remain close to the energies of Earth and Gaia in order to assist the ascension process of both Gaia and humanity from the "other side." In one of our Spiritual Research Group sessions, Archangel Michael clarified our understanding of the role of Ascended Masters:

> *The definition and title of Ascended Master is not used in discussions beyond Earth. However, it has been necessary for us to find ways to categorize, define certain beings, certain events so that your logic, your need for a certain level of information is met. Those that we classify as an Ascended Master are not defined strictly by their level of consciousness. They are a group of beings who are deeply committed to Earth Ascension and Humanity's Ascension, and have taken on different jobs to assist that process, including some of them spending time incarnated on Earth so they have a better knowledge of the experience. Some of them come from very high frequencies of consciousness; others are significant, but their gifts lie in other areas and they are on their own ascension path. An Ascended Master carries with them an individual, unique gift package and their willingness to commit to serving Gaia and human ascension.*

> *Obviously, Earth is commanding a great deal of attention. However, beings like myself have other jobs, other activities, other areas that we tend to that have nothing to do with Earth, commitments we have taken on, which does not diminish our concern and our interest in Earth's ascension. Ascended Masters have committed the bulk of their life energies and focus for the duration of Gaia's ascension and*

humans' ascension, to assisting that project. They have taken that on in a similar fashion to those humans, those souls who have committed to incarnating on Earth through the ascension process to be here at this time to assist.

Presently there are many Ascended Masters assisting the current ascension process on Earth described in Tolle's *A New Earth*. Examples of Ascended Masters include St. Germain, Lady Kwan Yin, Jesus/Sananda, Lord Buddha, and Kuthumi; many others have come to help from other worlds and dimensions. A full description of the mission and functions of each Ascended Master is contained in Schroeder's *"Ascended Masters and Their Retreats."*

Group Consciousnesses. A Group Consciousness (or Cluster Consciousness, Collective Consciousness, etc.) may be formed whenever two or more spiritual beings determine that their interests, objectives and energetic signatures or levels are in harmony. Additionally, there seems to be no upper limit to the number of members within a Group Consciousness.

In a Group Consciousness that provides information through a verbal Channel, all the members of the group are in constant and simultaneous energetic communication with each other, allowing the group to come to a consensus for the spokesperson to transfer information telepathically to the Higher Self of the Channel. Sometimes a collective may choose to identify themselves with a specific name, such as Flora, or they may simply identify themselves as The Collective, The Arcturians, The Federation of Light, The Council, or other collective names. Whether contact is made with a Group Consciousness Being or with an individual spiritual being (e.g., Higher Self, Ascended Master, Archangel, etc.), it is very important to positively ascertain that the level of consciousness of the being or beings with whom you are in contact is at least Fifth-Dimensional, and preferably higher. (See Appendix B).

The group consciousness entities with whom our Spiritual Research Group has communicated have explained that our linear physical brains are constructed in a way that allows only a single communication to be perceived and interpreted at a time, whereas a group consciousness can simultaneously listen to and interpret several different energetic conversations from different beings. Examples of cluster consciousnesses we have worked with include a representative of the Andazi Civilization which visited Earth long ago, a spokesperson for the Galactic Federation of Planets which represents several extraterrestrial civilizations, and a cluster consciousness composed of several Spirit Guides; each is discussed below.

The Andazi Civilization. In Robert Shapiro's 2013 book *The Explorer Race*, he mentioned an extremely ancient race called the Andazi that had visited Earth many millennia ago. Since I had not heard of this civilization before, I enlisted the help of my Spiritual Research Group. When I asked for a representative of the Andazi Civilization to come forward, a being appeared and, after being properly challenged, it announced in a very authoritative voice, "We are of the Andazi!" When I asked what his name was, he said that I could not understand his speech and that I should suggest a name. He immediately accepted the name "Talbot" and offered that he had evolved to the point where he was actually androgynous and whose Home World was in the Milky Way Galaxy, but it had been destroyed by cosmic incidents and space debris long ago.

Talbot also mentioned that communicating like this through a being in such a lower dimension of consciousness (the Channel was in her Spiritual Area in the Fifth Dimension of

Consciousness) was "a new concept for us" and "we are somewhat interested in the process of individual identity." With his continuing use of the plural "we" and "our," I took this to mean that he was normally in simultaneous telepathic communication with others of his race, wherever they were, and that individual identity was, to him, a curious characteristic of our 3D world. He further stated, "We had evolved to the point of not necessarily needing continuous existence in a specific location..." and had evolved into the ability to translate in and out of a corporeal existence, and then had evolved further.

Galactic Federation of Planets. In my 2017 book *The ETs Speak: Who We Are And Why We're Here*, to better understand the purpose and mission of the daily presence and observation of their spacecraft or Unidentified Flying Objects in our skies, I separately interviewed Nu-Mon and Kyton, representatives of the Galactic Federation, as well as spokespersons for six individual extraterrestrial (ET) civilizations. The information provided through at least two different Channels is from the representative of each of the six civilizations, as well as from the Galactic Federation. Although the information is not precisely identical in the minute details, it was remarkably similar in the general theme and message given from the various civilization's representatives. In each case, the spokesperson was speaking for, and with the instantaneous telepathic assistance and support of, the civilization they represented (Pleiadians, Arcturians, Antareans, Sirians, the Blue Avians and The Greys, etc.); in addition, the Andromedan representatives were interviewed from within their own Galaxy regarding their participation and support for the Galactic Federation within our Milky Way Galaxy.

Spirit Guides. One of the experienced Channels in our Spiritual Research Group reported that, when she was in her Spiritual Area, her awareness 'became that of her Higher Self,' where she was known as Hylia, and Agnes was her individual Spirit Guide. During a later session, Agnes announced that she was now within a group of four other Guides with a similar purpose and energetic level of evolution, and that her new Cluster Consciousness would act as Hylia's Spirit Guide from that time forward. When I asked the spokesperson for the group what name I should now address her by, she replied that each member of her cluster was like the individual petals of a beautiful flower, so I should call her Flora.

The Multi-Dimensional Higher Self. Every human being has an eternal spiritual essence that temporarily inhabits their physical body, an energetic essence that we usually call their Soul or their Higher Self. This spiritual essence was created as an individuated spark of the Soul consciousness created by the One Infinite Creator and the Elohim to explore and experience through repeated physical manifestations (incarnations) the universe and all of its varied creations. The purpose of these repeated trips through physical lifetimes is to experience all of life in all its variations, thus allowing the One Infinite Creator to add to Its knowledge of what It is. In one of our Spiritual Research Group sessions, I asked one of my students, Karen (not her real name), to move her conscious awareness from this third-dimensional reality into her "Spiritual Area" and there, as Anaka, her fifth-dimensional Higher Self personality, to describe who and what she was and what she experienced in her 'higher' spiritual realms of awareness as a conscious energetic being; this is an excerpt of her own description of herself as a Higher Self:

I am what you may think of as the personification of consciousness, the individualized piece of energy of Source Itself that has exhibited as my particular self. I am the voice of the energetic entity that expresses in three dimensions as Karen (not her real name). *I am that connection between All That Is and the representation of Source that is Karen. I am the energy that sends her what is described as "nudges" or "ideas." I am her reminder of her divinity, of her being only a part of and representation of All That Is. I am her source of living energy. I am associated with all other energies of All That Is, but my focus is on Anaka and Karen.*

My greater purpose within this lifetime is to expand my energetic knowledge of All That Is, to assist in the raising of vibration of all of humanity's consciousness within this lifetime, at this time. This is a time in which many Souls' Higher Selves have a much greater ability to influence the whole than has been available in the past, as there are many more Higher Selves that have made themselves available and have tapped into the energy of All That Is, and are aware of each other within that energy, giving strength to that energy.

I have prepared through many, many, many lifetimes on Earth, going through many different lessons, being on both sides of what is the division within third dimension (male and female), seeing what is in third dimension considered "good" and considered "bad" as lives, so that I was able to serve as a "victim", and as well serve as a "perpetrator" upon that victim, and therefore can access what is behind motivation on both sides of that. So, the lives that I have chosen up to this point have been working toward increasing my understanding of and connection with how third dimension physicality works, while maintaining a connection in whatever way I could to my soul energy that is on the other side of the Veil. I have had lives where I have been persecuted for my beliefs; I have also had lives where I have been able to maintain my beliefs; and I have had lives where I have given up my beliefs in fear of losing my life. So, I have trained through many lifetimes to be able to calmly proceed forward without fear in this lifetime.

When asked if she, as her Higher Self, was able to consciously interact with other beings in the spiritual realms; she replied:

We all have access to those on the other side, including Masters and Angels and Archangels, Seraphim, etc., and they have access to us. Often, in third dimension, the entity within third dimension is skeptical of information that may come in from the outside, not realizing that it may be information important for their growth, and so they block it because it is "unknown" or "unseen" and therefore they are suspicious. But Angels, Masters, Archangels, etc. are always watching and not really manipulating, but rather sending energy and sending Love and sending ideas that may be helpful. As Earth is very quickly changing right now, it has brought a lot of attention from all of those on the other side, including higher dimensional extra-terrestrials, who have come to give energy, and to assist in any way that is accepted. That energetic help must be received and accepted by third dimensional entities to be used, but it always there and always available.

More and more, third dimensional humans are now

becoming fourth dimensional and even recognizing their fifth dimensionality, and by doing so, they are opening avenues of communication that were previously closed, and because of that, more and more information is flooding in, is being observed by those not receiving it but who are open to reception of it, and they also begin to receive. So, that information is there and available, not necessarily tapped into, but is being enhanced and enlarged in the amount of what we see as "time" goes forward. So, we all have access to information from Angels, etc. and they can give us that information when we are ready to receive it.

When I asked Anaka if Joshua, her spirit Guide, was also always with her and available for consultation, Anaka replied through Karen:

You are now asking questions of perception within fifth and higher dimensions. Fifth dimensionally, yes, he is ALWAYS and forever with me, as there is nowhere else to be, except where All That Is exists, but my awareness of him comes and goes. He is always "with" me and my physical body, as my body is my soul's expression in her third dimensional existence. My conscious mind is not always thinking about Joshua, and is not always consciously aware that he is there. I would say I am always aware of my own beingness as Anaka, although Karen isn't always consciously thinking of herself as Anaka, but that is a goal.

For Joshua, as he is "busy" on the other side of the veil and has more than one responsibility, he is what you may think of as "multi-dimensional". I am aware that is where our conversation is going, that he is working from a multi-dimensional level. That is because he is multi-dimensional, and is consciously in contact with (beings of) whatever dimension he chooses to perceive. We could say that is one of the major differences between third dimensional and fifth dimensional and higher, is that in the higher dimensions have extremely blurry lines between dimensions. That is part of higher dimensionality, the ability to be conscious of and be within more than one dimension within consciousness, whereas in third and fourth dimension, we can tap into fifth dimensionality, we can be aware of fifth dimensionality, but we normally don't live within more than one dimension at a time. When we begin to describe it, it becomes more complicated when you get into higher dimensions, to describe exactly how multi-dimensionality works.

Joshua also assists when we bring in entities from other dimensions. You can remember that we have spoken with higher-dimensional extra-terrestrial people, who have said that they are ninth or twelfth or higher dimensionals, and they have been contacted with my Guide's ability to move between dimensions and bring their consciousness to fifth dimensionality to communicate with my physical body's consciousness.

As Anaka, I have the ability to be higher than fifth dimensional. This may sound strange, but it is now my time and space to be fifth dimensional while my physical body is third dimensional. As a fifth dimensional being, I am the focal point between third dimension and higher, and remain so in order to keep my physical body in contact with myself, Anaka, my fifth dimensional Higher Self. You might say I "ride the wave" of fifth dimension, so that I am very close to my third dimensional self, always right there in contact with my third dimensional self, while remaining fifth dimensional to be able to do so. At this point, I would prefer to be in contact with Karen's conscious mind all the time, as she is evolving very quickly now and needs consistent contact.

How much learning we have to look forward to!

Astral Entities. The Fourth Dimension of Consciousness (See Appendix B) is sometimes also called the Astral Realm. This is the realm or the spiritual 'space' in which your consciousness exists at night when you dream, when your awareness has temporarily moved out of the physical body. Here you can fly through the air or move through the oceans or even visit other worlds as pure consciousness, yet you will always maintain an essential energetic connection that allows you to return to your physical body when you're through dreaming and it's time to wake up.

The energies you become aware of in the astral realms include not only the vibrations of the conscious thoughtforms you resonate with; they can also include conscious energetic thoughtforms external to your own mind that are drawn to your vibrations and, if you allow them, can become temporarily or even permanently embedded in your own energy field.

Thoughtforms. There is a fundamental Law of Physics that says "Energy can neither be created nor destroyed – it can only change its form." Energy, in itself, is neutral – neither good nor bad; however, we 'color' the energy of our thoughts, words and actions with either the good or bad feelings and emotions attached to that energy. A thought carries with it a certain amount of energy, but the words we speak carry more energy than a mere thought, and an action carries even more energy than the words we speak. So, what happens to all that negative energy that you throw energy from your own energy field toward someone you hate through your thoughts, words and actions? (I'm going to hurt you because I hate you!) What happens to all that energy that you have colored as negative when you're afraid of something in the dark you can't see? (I'm afraid that might hurt me!) What happens to all that negative energy that you take in from others because you believe the incorrect negative or limiting thoughts of others? (Men are better than women!)

The vibrational energy of all the intentions and thoughts you create, the words you speak and the actions you take is added to your own energy field and, by extension, to the collective consciousness of all of humanity, to what the psychologist Carl Jung called "The Collective Unconscious". If those energies were low in vibrational frequency (hate, fear, anger, greed, etc.), they are added to the lower levels of the Fourth Dimensional Astral Realm. If those energies were high in vibrational frequency (e.g., love, compassion, beauty, harmony, etc.), they are added to the upper levels of the Fourth Dimensional Astral Realm.

What happens when you sleep at night and your awareness returns to the Fourth Dimension of consciousness, what do you dream of? Without your conscious mind to distract and focus you, the vibrational frequencies you have in your energy field are automatically drawn through harmonic resonance to similar frequencies in the Collective Consciousness of Humanity (e.g., Birds of a feather flock together), and you could become aware of the monsters, werewolves, and ghoulish residents of the lower levels of the Astral Realms. The remedy is, of course, to live your conscious life in at least the upper levels of the Fourth Dimension of Consciousness (see Appendix B).

Earth-Bound Entities (EBs). In his book *Spirit Releasement Therapy*, the late Dr. William Baldwin identified three types of negative conscious entities whose energies can become attached to or embedded in a person's own energy field, or aura, for the purpose of affecting their human behaviors: Earth-Bound Entities (EBs), Extraterrestrials (ETs), and Dark Force Entities (DFEs). Baldwin appears to assume that attached EBs are truly negative and harmful; however, in providing Past Life Regression and Regression Therapy to many clients of my own, a non-negative (not evil) consciousness can also attach to a person's energy field, and in fact, the human person can even *invite* a spiritual entity to become attached to their energies.

Examples include the case when a young mother died and chose to remain bound to the human auric energies of her children to make sure they were safe and protected. In another case, a grieving widow, whose husband 'graduated' two years prior, was still energetically holding onto the soul of her dead husband and not letting him go by keeping his ashes on the mantel, making sure his shirts were all freshly washed and ironed each week, and setting an empty place at the dinner table for him each evening. In the letter case, although the motivation may have not been harmful, the result was that the husband's soul who had left the physical body behind was negatively affected by remaining energetically connected to the lower (3D) dimension of his wife and not returning to the higher dimensions of existence. A conversation was begun with the wife's Higher Self and the husband's Earth-Bound soul, and the wife realized how she was harming her husband's own spiritual progress; with this realization, she quickly released her energetic connection while retaining the positive memories of their life together.

Extraterrestrials (ETs). Again, Baldwin appears to consider all extraterrestrials (ETs) as being negative in the sense of "evil"; however, this is not really the case. Yes, some ETs who are in the lower third and fourth dimensions of consciousness are what we would call "bad" in the sense that they are in service only to themselves as a domineering and/or conquering external force from space; however, through channeling sessions with our Spiritual Research Group, we have also met many "good" ETs who exist in and are telepathically visiting from the fifth and higher dimensions of consciousness. Several examples of this type of contact are described in my book *The ETs Speak: Who We Are and Why We're Here.* The difference is that the more spiritually evolved ETs act only in the greatest good of all concerned, rather than the "what's in it for me" or Service To Self mentality of third and/or lower fourth dimensional consciousness.

My first experience with an ET came in 2003 during a typical Past Life Regression session to release negative energy that caused a series of upsetting emotional reactions for my client over a period of about a year. While 'stirring up' the energy patterns in her Solar Plexus Chakra, I became aware of a communication device of some kind in her energy field that was linked to an ET scientist on a spacecraft. Using Baldwin's conversation protocol, the scientist informed me that an etheric device had been implanted in her energies that allowed them to experiment on her emotions. When they tweaked a dial on their spacecraft, it would cause an emotional reaction which they were then able to monitor. I then informed the ET that their experiment and all their experimental data was now invalid because we were aware of what they were doing, and commanded them to remove all devices and implants and leave our Solar System. Upon emerging from hypnosis, the client felt a great release and relief. Unfortunately, I did not have an opportunity for long-term follow up with this client because she soon moved, and I have had no further contact with her.

In "*The ETs Speak*" book, we have also become aware of some ETs with third dimensional consciousness (those little "Grays") who have, for unknown reasons, reportedly abducted humans for a short time and then returned them to their daily life. Since we have not clearly understood their reasons and motives for abducting humans, in our fear of what we don't understand, we have labelled them all as "bad." The above-mentioned book tells a much different story; instead of using hypnotic regression to determine why the client had been abducted, a hypnotic interview with the *abductors* (the Grays*)* showed that their motives were quite benign, but grossly misinterpreted by the alleged abductee. Instead, the ETs informed us that their intention was to gather and preserve human DNA so that humanity could be re-established on an appropriate planet following the nuclear destruction of Earth, which they took as a foregone conclusion from our previous misuse of nuclear weapons! The positive motive was clearly misunderstood, and has resulted in many Hollywood movies showing mass fear and hysteria about an ET invasion and takeover or destruction of humanity.

Dark Force Entities (DFEs). A Dark Force Entity is a being whose energetic consciousness is very low in vibratory frequency as a result of innumerable experiences that have taught it that it is very dark, full of hatred and anger and completely evil. As a result, it has lost its connection to Source which provides positive life force energy, and moves about in the lower Fourth Dimension of Consciousness looking for living victims that it can attach to and drain their energy in order to continue existing as a force of evil and darkness –

definitely not the spiritual sources that one would choose to connect with.

If the person's own vibratory frequency is very low to begin with (e.g., drug-dependent or filled with rage, hate and anger), they may also attract DFEs of similar vibratory frequencies during sleep when their consciousness returns to the Fourth Dimension at night. There is a good reason that loving parents teach their children bedroom prayers! The point here is that these DFE demonic energies are real, but are also easy to avoid when either consciously or unconsciously opening your energy field to contact the "other side"; the simple act of a loving prayer or intentional thought or word is enough to ensure that your vibrations remain high and that the negative energy of DFEs cannot approach.

One must also remember that even these conscious DFEs are also creations of the All That Is, even though the DFE may not believe or be aware of that. Baldwin offers a protocol for dealing with attached dark entities that may be encountered during, for example, an energy healing session, and I can attest that the protocol is effective for removing a demonic energy from a client. However, simply removing and banishing the DFE may be very healing for the client, but it only frees the DFE to search for and exploit another victim elsewhere. A better solution for the therapist is to use a modification of the technique developed by the Denver Hypnotherapist Greg McHugh. This process, described with McHugh's permission in my book, "*Trans-Scalar Healing*" (see Bibliography), not only removes the DFE from the client's energy field, but also provides the potential for healing the DFE with the active assistance of the Angelic Kingdom and allow it to return Home to the higher dimensions.

However, these conscious DFEs can sometimes be inadvertently attracted and attached when the living person's energy field is significantly weakened, such as during surgery under general anesthesia or following physical trauma, especially to the head, where the person experiences loss of consciousness. Another situation that can attract less desirable spiritual sources of information is when intentionally opening your energy field to "the other side" without energetically preparing yourself and clearly stating who you intend to connect with. Ouija Boards and other spiritual connection parlor games can, through your intentions or lack of intentions, connect to "someone" who would like to speak to humans, and evidently there are many in the lower levels of the Fourth Dimension of Consciousness who would jump at the chance. However, the information and guidance you may receive is limited by the experiences and wisdom of the source you connect to, so it makes sense to connect to and speak with only those whom you know to be reliable and trusted sources of information. I prefer to limit my metaphysical conversations to Creator, Archangels, Ascended Masters, Guides and Higher Selves.

The Akashic Record. The term "Akashic" comes from the Sanskrit word "Akasha" meaning "etheric" or "of the unseen ethers." The Akashic Record is a term popularized by the early 20th century psychic Edgar Cayce to mean the etheric source of all information he received unconsciously while in an extremely deep state of self-hypnosis. In order to find the source or cause of his inability to speak, he was taught by a traveling Stage Hypnotist how to place himself into a state of very deep physical and mental relaxation that was so profound that he had no conscious memory of what he did or said while in that state; however, when in that state, he was able to clearly speak the answer to any question that was asked of him by Gladys Davis, his trusted secretary and assistant. Cayce's fame grew quickly as he was initially able, while self-hypnotized, to determine both the cause and cure of any physical illness or condition that was presented to him, yet he later had no conscious recollection or memory of any of the information he provided.

By the 1940's Cayce's interest had primarily shifted from helping to relieve or cure physical diseases to investigating more esoteric metaphysical and spiritual topics such as the soul, the afterlife, Atlantis, and other physical and non-physical beings that exist in this and other Galaxies throughout the cosmos. The Akashic Record is, of course, the ultimate library or source of information that may be accessed for learning and guidance about any object or event in Creation. Cayce's secretary, Gladys, recorded and transcribed all the thousands of Cayce's channeled session he called 'readings,' and this body of information has been archived in the Edgar Cayce Foundation's Association For Research And Enlightenment (The A.R.E.) in Virginia Beach, VA. A much more complete history and account of this remarkable psychic pioneer can be found in the many biographies that have been published about his lifetime works, such as Jess Stearn's "*The Sleeping Prophet*" and Thomas Sugrue's "*There Is A River*".

In the previous century, the Akashic Records had been thought to hold sacred information and, therefore, only a very few people with advanced psychic abilities had gained access to its contents; however, with more and more people now beginning to awaken to their innate spiritual abilities, the prior limitations on access have been removed. Anyone who understands that the Akashic Record is the complete record of all experiences in the universe is now allowed access to this truly universal history.

The contents of the Akashic Record are infinite and record the vibrational signature of all thoughts ever thought, all deeds ever done, and all objects and events ever created by any physical or non-physical being in this and all other Universes. Such an immense body of information and knowledge is simply not comprehensible by the human brain, but we humans are not required to even attempt to do so. It is enough for us to realize that there is an answer to any question we can pose, or even imagine, if it is important that we know the answer.

For us to be able to visualize, understand and access this huge library of information, The Akashic Record can be considered to be in the form of a Book of All Knowledge, with Part 1 discussing the entire spiritual knowledge and memory of every individual's current and previous physical lifetimes, as well as their spiritual non-physical experiences between physical lifetimes (the Personal Akashic Record), and Part 2 discussing everything else (Universal Akashic Records). These are discussed below, as well as the conditions which must be met for accessing the information in either the Personal or Universal Akashic Records.

The Personal Akashic Record. Each sentient human and non-human being has associated with them a complete record of their vibrational energies, the energetic memories of every thought, action and deed throughout all their experiences, both while incarnated and not incarnated, since their eternal soul was given individual awareness of itself by Creator. However, while incarnated in a human body, the human brain and its associated consciousness (Ego) is usually unable to connect with and recall these spiritual experiences or memories prior to the time when the human child was about five or six years old. This is the average age of a child when they become aware that they are an individual personality separate from their mother, the age at which their own ego begins to assert its own reasoning powers, when their *conscious memories* begin to form as a result of only what they have experienced through their five physical senses from that time forward in their current lifetime.

There are very few people who can remember their third birthday party, or the gifts they received, or the color of the dress or shirt they wore, yet they know they had a third birthday and received gifts. However, these experiences can all be clearly recalled under hypnosis. This forms the foundational strength of hypnosis as an effective therapeutic approach to discovering and understanding the cause of many emotional and/or physical traumas that may continue to negatively affect the personal and social interactions of the child as they grow through adolescence into adulthood. Once the causative factors are understood, appropriate therapeutic remedies and protocols can be provided to restore the person to a more balanced and productive lifetime.

The objectives of hypnotic techniques and processes are to bypass the analytical decision-making functions of the thinking mind and its ego (Is this True or False? Safe or Not Safe?) and to allow access to the part of one's mind (the Subconscious Mind) that can access are recall ALL the person's experiences. This is how Edgar Cayce initially was able to recall, albeit unconsciously, the appropriate information stored in his client's Personal Akashic Record, and also later esoteric and metaphysical information from the Universal Akashic Record. This is also what happens when a trained Hypnotherapist provides a Past Life Regression for his or her client.

The Universal Akashic Record. The Universal Akashic Record contains the vibrational signature of every event and occurrence, not associated with an individual's Personal Akashic Record, that has ever happened in this

Universe, as well as all events that, based on current events and intentions, have a high probability of occurring in the near future. However, the farther out into the future one peers, the more unreliable the information becomes, since the future also hold the possibility that a choice in the actions associated with current events could result in a different outcome (future).

In my previous book *Spiritual Journeys*, our Spiritual Research Group has investigated the information contained in the current Akashic Records regarding a very wide spectrum of topics, including the nature of the spiritual realms of existence, who made the Crop Circles seen around the world and why were they made, Life in Atlantis, how the Egyptian pyramids were built and by whom, the nature of the Elemental Kingdom, and many other topics. Our Spiritual Research Group has also investigated the pre-historic sunken Yonoguni Monument off the coast of Japan, other lifeforms within our Solar System, inter-species communications with animals and dolphins, the UFO presence and activities in our Solar System, as well as details on many additional subjects. The above-mentioned book, *The ETs Speak*, documents conversations with several extra-solar civilizations within our own and neighboring galaxies.

Conditions For Access. Information and details on virtually any subject or topic in the entire Akashic Record are readily available under the right conditions. However, information will not be automatically provided; although the Good Book promised, "Ask and ye shall receive," it did not include the fine print. Again, we have found that answers to our questions will always be provided if: One - we are ready to understand the information (our vocabulary includes words and comprehensible concepts about the information received); Two - receiving the information will be in the highest and best good of all concerned (Sorry, you won't get next week's lottery numbers); and Three – the information will not cause harm of any kind to any living being, including yourself. Once these three conditions are met, we have always received answers to our inquiries, along with an infinite amount of patience from our Higher Self, Spirit Guide, or other assisting agent, to assist in our comprehension of the information.

Depending on the nature of the information one is looking for, different spiritual helpers are available to assist in accessing the information. If you are looking for details about any subject or experience that your Higher Self has participated in, the information is in your own soul record, and your Higher self always has access to that information, subject to the above conditions. Additionally, if you are looking for solid information about events or experiences in the future (e.g., When will Disclosure about the presence of UFOs occur?), you will probably be politely informed that the probability of future events actually happening depends primarily on what we collectively or individually choose to do today. And occasionally, we are told politely that specific answers to some questions will not be provided at this time because knowing the timing of a future event might disrupt the sequence of other events that must happen first for an event to have the desired result.

However, if you are looking for information that your soul has not witnessed or participated in (e.g., Who made the crop circles and why? How many solar systems in our Milky Way Galaxy now support intelligent life? etc.), your Spirit Guide is a better choice to help you gain access to that information. In addition, your Guide will know if the above conditions have been met, and will also know if there are any limitations that should be imposed on that access.

Co-Habitation. Co-habitation is defined as the experience of simultaneously having several consciousnesses "present" in the expanded awareness of the Channel during a Spiritual Research Group session. In all directed verbal channeling sessions conducted with one of our trained Channels, we have always begun with the Channel's Higher Self being present, and this is then normally followed by inviting the Channel's Spirit Guide to come forward as well and announce their presence. By default, the Director's Higher Self and Spirit Guide are always present in all conversations, and may also be invited to participate as appropriate. Additional "guests," such as a Group Consciousness Entity, an Ascended Master or an Archangel, can also be invited to offer information on specific topics within their expertise (e.g. Archangel Raphael for healing). Therefore, it is necessary to have a protocol for managing the conversation so that a coherent transcript that properly identifies the source speaking may be produced for the session.

After calling an entity forward, and ensuring that they really are who we call forward, it is appropriate that all entities be asked to come forward and speak one at a time when requested to offer their information and wisdom. This is required because the Higher Self of the Channel must telepathically receive and comprehend the information presented by the Source, and then translate that "instantaneous energetic package" of information, imagery, and feelings into the vocabulary and language of the Channel.

If the source of the information is a Collective or Group Consciousness, the collective's spokesperson must additionally integrate all the simultaneous information offered by each member of the collective, and telepathically present a single consensus information package to the Higher Self of the Channel. The Channel's physical brain and neurological pathways must then accurately interpret the telepathic transmission received from their Higher Self, so it can verbally relay the interpreted information to the Director of the session.

So, what does the Channel feel when more than one Source is "present" during a directed verbal channeling? As expected, different Channels will have different experiences. One experienced Channel stated that she did not experience any differences between when several entities were 'present' and when there was only a single entity 'present'. During the development of *"The ETs Speak: Who We Are And Why We're Here,"* another experienced Channel described it like this:

Well, I find that it can feel a little bit crowded. I can have three or four beings present at once, and all of their energy is enveloping me at once, it all kind of blends together, but when one being is invited to step forward and speak, the rest of the people would still be there, still be listening, and I would still feel their energy. And it really depends on who is present. My Guide can appear visually as a physical being, but normally he is energetic, always there, but not pushing out energy all the time. Archangel Michael is always pushing out energy, always, and Ashtar is one of my favorites because his energy is so positive, so golden, so honest-feeling. And when we called the first Gray in, I could tell he didn't want to come – his energy kind of held back a little, just enough to tell me, "I'm not available to you, but another could be. It is possible to do this, but not with me" kind of feeling. But then, the second Gray came, and she felt very wise, very old, very gentle and soft, and very knowledgeable, like "OK, I'm the one you can ask questions to". And the Pleiadians feel very "homey", very familiar, like if you went back to your old neighborhood and talked to

*people there, you kind of feel comfortable. The
Arcturians are like old friends that live far away, kind of
feeling. And sometimes when a different being is
called forward to speak through me, I feel my body
jerk or move, and I feel it in the chair, and it's kind of
like an adjustment, or a little twist of the energy. And
every now and then when I am channeling, I can
almost feel my mind saying, "What? Really?" That
kind of feeling, but it's way in the back, like I'm not
unconscious, but I'm not totally involved in the
conversation. When I'm channeling, I feel like I'm in a
different space in my Higher Self, but when I meditate,
I don't feel like I go into my Higher Self. When I'm
channeling I feel as if I'm a conduit for information
from a higher Source than from my mind, but when I'm
meditating, I'm still asking for and receiving
information, but I don't feel like a conduit.*

The Telepathic Connection. As mentioned in the
Introduction, the process that we humans use for channeling is
initially extremely cumbersome for non-physical sources who
have not regularly used this communication modality before.
In addition, many sources have reported that for them, it is
extremely difficult for them to maintain a telepathic connection
to the Channel's Higher Self if the physical Channel cannot
raise their awareness to at least the Fifth Dimension of
consciousness. Several sources have stated that, in spite of the
energetic difficulties of lowering their own vibrations down to
the Fifth Dimension of consciousness to telepathically
exchange information with the Channel at that level, they are
eager to learn and practice this "new" ability for them. In
addition, they are grateful for the opportunity to make a
connection with those humans who are able to raise their
vibrations to 5D, even if just for a short time. Several spiritual
beings have even requested patience and understanding on our

beyond that of just sending a telepathic thought from the Sender to the Receiver, as illustrated in this example:

> *Being: We often communicate just by instantaneous exchanges of energy which are known by the other person or group of beings with whom we are communicating. It is a very difficult process to explain in words. It is an immediate knowing of information exchange that happens so fast that, using your timeline terminology, one does not even know it is happening – they are just suddenly doing, thinking or working with the new information. It is an exchange of a universally understood energy code, would be the best way to explain it to you, almost as if there were a universal language because energy has its own signatures for whatever is being transmitted. All understand what that transmission or energy means, and act accordingly. What is important is that I have a clear pathway for energy transmission so that I might provide what I am witnessing, translating, etc. In talking to you now, you are hearing and translating in your mind the words that are coming through to you. Those words carry an energy signature that not only comes to you, to your hearing system and to your translation system and your brain, but that energy signature surrounds and interacts with the environment as well. When, for example, you talk about prayer circles, one reason that those prayers for healing work so well is because that energy has been released into what you would call the cosmos, and that energy changes patterns of surrounding energy. Is this helping? Are you understanding?*

However, this process occurs instantaneously in the spiritual realms between the Source and Higher Self participants, regardless of where the Sender and Receiver are 'located', and it is enough for us to know that it always happens even beyond our need to understand, at this time, how it happens.

Chapter 3
Exploring Your Spiritual Area

Chapter 1 provided a general overview and sampling of the wide variety of techniques and modalities that are available to begin investigating and expressing the spiritual side of one's being, as well as some of the considerations involved in that investigation. Chapter 2 provided some insights into the spectrum of conscious spiritual beings with whom a conversation may be established, as well as a few recommendations on which classes of beings should be sought out, and which ones should be avoided. With this background, this chapter examines in much greater detail the various modalities I have actually practiced, experienced and found useful for expanding my own conscious awareness into my Spiritual Area. From there, I can then explore and use the several spiritual abilities that are available. Again, these are examples of the techniques along my own pathway of investigation and learning that I have been drawn to, but you should use your own discernment to decide if they are appropriate and relevant to your pathway and desired experiences.

Expanding Your Awareness

In order to explore your Spiritual Area, you must first be able to expand your conscious awareness into at least the 5th Dimension of consciousness, the beginning level where your conscious awareness becomes that of your Higher Self. As discussed in Chapter 1, there are many methods of doing this; however, not all techniques or modalities have worked for me, so I would like to provide some examples from my own experience that have taught me how to take this important step. I have found two types of techniques that allowed me to access my Spiritual Area – techniques that involve guided visualization and imagery, and techniques that involve self-hypnotic processes, and I will discuss examples of each below.

However, before I provide these examples, I need to address one important question: "Regardless of the method used to gain access to the Spiritual Area, how will I know – how can I *really* be sure - that I am all the way 'up there' in my Spiritual Area?" When I began my attempts to explore my Spiritual Area, I had obviously never been there before, so my logical, engineering-trained left brain did not have any memory of what it felt like, looked like, sounded like, etc. to actually BE in an expanded state of conscious awareness. There was nothing in my memory to compare what I was feeling at the time with what I thought my Spiritual Area really felt like, or even with what it 'should' feel like, and this began to cause a bit of fear and doubt in my mind that I could really do it.

Then I remembered that in my Hypnotherapeutic training, I learned that it is only the Ego, the thinking/analyzing part of the conscious mind, that can doubt. (See Eckert Tolle's "*A New Earth.*") Doubting is the Ego's job – to analyze every situation you meet, and assess whether or not it is safe or dangerous to proceed, to determine whether something is good or bad for you. And if it doesn't have enough information to determine that it positively is safe (such as when you have no prior memory of your Spiritual Area), the conscious mind automatically goes into the default mode of thinking that it is NOT safe or it is dangerous, and you had better not even try to take that leap into the unknown.

Fortunately, in the English language, there is a word that allows the conscious mind to ignore the doubt and fear of failure that the Ego may cause, and that magic word is "Pretend". We used that word all the time when we were children, so why did we stop using it? I decided that in my efforts to gain access to my

Spiritual Area and explore all the anticipated wonders there, I would begin by pretending that every word I heard when I listened to a meditation or guided imagery CD was absolutely true, and I could trust it completely. Of course, my fully conscious mind had already determined that the CD was safe and beneficial or at least pleasant, or I would not have bought it. So, pretending was not only allowed, it was encouraged! And that was when my efforts began to have tangible, realized results.

Conscious Guided Visualization. Most "New Age" bookstores carry a line of relaxing music and meditation CDs that involve a process of creating a tranquil walk through a forest, or feeling the ocean waves splash on your feet, or relaxing in a pleasant meadow on a warm sunny day. These guided visualization journeys are usually very pleasant and effective for creating a sense of peace and/or a feeling of quiet contemplation within, but in all the many meditation workshops I attended, I have found none that would carry my imagining mind all the way 'up' into my Spiritual Area... until I experienced Rev. Paul Soloman's Seven Terraces Meditation.

ILC Meditation. When I was in Virginia Beach from 1995-1998, I attended the Fellowship of the Inner Light Church, and its minister, Rev. Thomas Keller, was holding classes in what he called the Inner Light Consciousness (ILC) Meditation technique. This particular meditation technique is an adaptation of The Seven Terraces Meditation developed by the late Rev. Paul Solomon, who had founded that church several years before.

In Rev. Solomon's Seven Terraces Meditation workshops, it was stressed that this meditation must be practiced at least once each day for 40 *consecutive* days, and if you miss a day or go to sleep, you get to start all over. To Rev. Solomon, the significance of 40 days is that it represents (at least in Christian philosophy) a complete new beginning or renewal, as in "Noah's flood of 40 days and 40 nights," and Jesus' returning from the desert after 40 days of being challenged. For this reason, Rev. Solomon sometimes called this meditation the "40-Day Journey". However, as a Hypnotherapist, I know the wisdom of continued repetition to firmly embed the symbology and its meaning into the subconscious mind. And yes, listening to the same recording day after day for forty days gets fairly monotonous, but diligent patience has its own reward, as you will see below. I restarted after missing day three, and managed to complete the next 40 consecutive days.

The concept that drew me to the Inner Light Consciousness Meditation technique was that it did not ask me to empty my active mind and open to the vast grandeur of the universe; instead, it enlisted the mind's unlimited creative energy to provide an image-rich visual experience that led me through a beautiful meadow where my inner senses were awakened, across a bridge from the physical world into my spiritual world, up my own spiritual mountain, and into the Temple at the top where I could remember and connect with my own innate inner spiritual abilities.

The following description of the ILC Meditation sequence is fairly detailed, and I will highlight much of the symbology of this Journey without any apologies for its length, simply because I have found this one meditation technique to be most effective for moving my awareness into a profoundly expanded state of spiritual awareness. Having investigated many different approaches for reaching my Spiritual Area, this is the one meditation technique that has resulted in the deepest (or highest) experience for me; however, you will need to decide if it is the one that you choose to pursue. I can only describe my experience, not yours, but because of its effectiveness for me, the ILC Meditation has become the foundation for all the subsequent spiritual investigations that I have documented in the books I have written, including this one.

The guided imagery of the Inner Light Consciousness Meditation has been carefully crafted to provide the meditator with a meaningful and spiritually rich set of visualization and imagery cues that define a journey from your day-to-day physical consciousness into your Spiritual Area and back again. It is important that your experiences and insights of each spiritual journey are always brought back into your conscious world so you can integrate this new knowledge into your conscious daily activities. This journey up my spiritual mountain allowed me to awaken my inner senses, bridge the duality of mind, integrate my entire energy system (chakras, meridians and bodies), and enter my 'inner temple' at the top of the mountain, where I learned how to heal myself and others, read my own Personal Akashic Record, and enter a profoundly deep meditative state.

The ILC Meditation begins with several guided visualization images that promote relaxing the physical body into a very safe place, the "Point Of Perfect Balance," that safe place within yourself where you know that all is well. When you are ready, you then move from your physical body into your Meadow, a near-universal metaphor for a place of peace and tranquility, where you learn to heighten and expand your inner senses of physical awareness. Feel the reality of your meadow -- feel it, see it, taste it, hear it, and smell it and breathe it all in as you smile pleasantly at the blue sky and the white clouds above, and actually feel the warmth of the sun on your skin. Feel the grass as it tingles beneath your bare feet, be very aware of all the brilliant colors of the wild flowers, smell their sweet fragrance, and reach down to touch the silky petal of a beautiful flower.

Somewhere in your meadow there will always be a field of corn. It may be very large or quite small, but corn is a near-global symbol of abundance and plenty, and since this corn is in your meadow, the corn is all yours, so you are free to pick as much abundance as you wish and take it with you. All of life's abundance is right here in your own cornfield, available for the taking any time you wish. As you exit the corn field, you come to a fruit tree that is full and ripe with your favorite fruit, and you just know it will taste juicy and delicious. Notice the fruit and its inviting color, touch and feel the rough tree bark and feel the weight and size of the fruit in your hand, and as you bite into the fruit, savor its succulent juices and the smooth taste of its delicious sweetness in your mouth.

As you finish eating your fruit, you will hear the bubbling and gurgling of a clear mountain stream in the distance. As you walk toward it and kneel down by its banks to wash the sticky fruit juice from your hands, gaze into the running waters and let your consciousness extend into the waters so you can feel the energies and the strength there. The river with its bubbling waters is a reflection of your spiritual energy, your own life force energies, at that time. Become very familiar with the way they feel to you.

As you look up from the river, notice a bridge that crosses over the river. Just take a moment to see what it looks like to you: what it is made of, how long it is, how high it is, and how it is constructed. You should record these mental notes in your journal when you finish the meditation. You may find that it begins to appear differently or has different construction characteristics as you proceed through your 40-day Journey. The bridge is the subconscious symbol that represents the separation between the physical and spiritual portions of your consciousness, and the length of the bridge represents the degree of separation between the physical and spiritual realms of your awareness.

As you cross the bridge over the mountain stream, you will see your spiritual mountain in the distance and a pathway that leads from the bridge toward your mountain. As you proceed along your pathway, notice that it takes you through several terraces or gardens, each of which has a different color. The first terrace is the Red Garden, the second is the Orange Garden, the third is the Yellow Garden, and so on. Each of these gardens has a different vibration, a higher vibration than the previous one. This journey through the gardens is also an energetic journey up through your own chakra system, and each terrace embodies a different lesson or the purpose as you climb toward the mountaintop.

The Red Garden is the Garden of Expectancy. Here you want to create a sense of anticipation and expectancy without expecting anything specific to happen, except that you <u>will</u> be changed as a result of this experience. Its mantra is "I know I will be changed by this experience!" Notice that everything in the garden is colored red – the trees, the rocks, the earth, everything is red. Feel the energies of the Red Garden, and really get into the feeling of expectancy for a moment.

The Orange Garden is the Garden of Transformation, where we realize that what we could not do yesterday is now within our reach today. Everything in the garden is colored orange, and its mantra is "I leave behind what I was yesterday, and I now open to what I can become!"

The Yellow Garden is the Garden of New Birth, Expansiveness and Joy. It is here that you can experience the expansiveness and joy of living a full, creative, joyous and productive life.

Everything is colored Yellow, and its mantra is "I look forward to my new life and to what lies ahead!"

As you begin walking along the pathway, notice that it now becomes much steeper. This is symbolic of leaving behind the three lower terraces (chakras) that relate to the physical body; you are now approaching the Green Garden, the doorway or Gateway to the upper three terraces (chakras) that relate to the spiritual aspects of your being. The journey now becomes more demanding, and the pathway becomes steeper.

As you enter the green Garden of The Companion, notice a brilliant being of light approaching you from the deep green forest. This is your Higher Self -- total, unconditional Love coming to greet you. Here, your mantra is "I don't know exactly who or what you are, but I simply want to know you better." And you *know* that this Companion will always be there walking with you; you *know* that you never have been and never will be alone – your Companion is always there for you.

The Blue Garden is the Garden of Communion, where you reach that point in your life's spiritual journey where you are content to be alone with your Companion, sharing and blending your energies with each other, knowing that there is nothing you want to hide or need to hide. Your mantra is "My Companion and I are One!" When you feel these energies here in your Blue Garden, you will again see your pathway continuing a bit steeper on up the mountainside.

The Violet Garden is the Garden of Responsibility; everything is colored Violet, and your mantra is "I accept the responsibility to use my talents and abilities wisely." With reverence, awe, and gratitude, accept the gifts and the information that is offered to you, and the abilities that will be needed to help you express your essence on the earth plane in the way you have chosen to meet your own challenges and lessons. Here, you may want to say to your Creator, "Thy will be done." But Creator will say back to you, "Oh, no! You're missing the meaning of your life if you turn it all over to me! What do YOU want? THY will be done!"

As you look upward, the mountaintop is still obscured in clouds and your pathway is not clear. But when you connect with the feeling of gratitude for this experience and accept the responsibility for your words, thoughts and actions, the clouds part and the loving hands of Creator lift you up and gently set you down in your White Garden.

The seventh terrace, the White Garden, is the Garden of Enlightenment, and is symbolic of your own inner sacred space, your Temple within that is not made with hands, the garden of limitless power, absolute harmony, and eternal duration. There in your White Garden is your Temple, your own personal sacred space within where the real power and effectiveness of the Inner Light Consciousness Meditation can be realized.

The Temple Experience is the pinnacle of your meditation. When you have prepared yourself to enter your Temple and then consciously choose to enter into your own sacred place within, you are truly standing in your own divine energy, your creative essence through which you can accomplish the goals of your meditation time. As you proceed toward your Temple, you will first come upon a clear, reflecting pool of water.

When you look down into it, you can see yourself very clearly in the reflection. Then, as you step down into the reflecting pool and walk along its bottom, you are metaphorically cleansing yourself. Here, all your thoughts are known, and you cannot ignore any facet of your personality; you must accept everything that you know yourself to be, and then ask silently that anything that is not in service to the Light be washed away from you, and leave you cleansed and purified. As you climb out of the reflecting pool on the other side you will see that everything that you are, even your clothes, are now washed and made pure – so pure that you radiate a white light outward for all to see.

As you enter your Temple, the first thing you see is a tall violet flame rising up from a square inscribed in the vestibule floor. This is the eternal flame of purification and transmutation which burns forever in your own spiritual essence. In the infinitely high vibrations of its perfect light, no lower vibrations can exist. As you step into this flame for a moment, any remaining impurities within you (such as lower or base thoughts, feelings or intentions) are immediately transmuted into a lump of gold which appears on the floor beside you. Now step out of the Violet Flame of Transmutation, pick up this gold, take it to the altar there in the center of your Temple, and offer it as a symbol of letting go of all your impurities, and also as a symbol of newly purified material with which to expand this Temple not made with hands.

As you rise, look around your Temple and see that there are three rooms that you may visit for various purposes. The first room you visit is your Healing Room. As you enter, you are greeted by Archangel Raphael, the Archangel of healing, harmony and balance. Here you can bring healing to the physical, emotional, mental and spiritual levels of yourself or, with their permission, another person. You embrace Archangel Raphael with a big hug, and then tell him that you are here just now on your 40-day journey and that you will return to your Healing Room when you are ready to begin your healing work.

The next room you will visit is the Hall Of Records that contains the Personal Akashic Records of all persons who have ever lived on the earth. You are greeted by your Record Keeper; he is the one to whom you will make your request for a specific record and who will retrieve and deliver the record to you. But for now, you will just give him a big hug, and tell him that you are here on your 40-day journey and that you will return when you are ready access and read your own personal Akashic Record or, if appropriate and with their permission, the Akashic Record of another person.

The last of the three rooms you will visit on your 40-day journey is your Meditation Room. Inside this pleasant, inviting space is a comfortable reclining chair in the center of the dimly-lit room. You will sit down in the chair, relax and allow your consciousness to expand into the experience, knowledge and information that the universe has to offer you at that time. This experience is a powerful meditation within a meditation.

After doing this meditation every day for about 30 days, a fourth room (the Learning Room) suddenly appeared right after I left the Hall of Records. As I entered The Learning Room, I saw what appeared to be my second-grade schoolroom with all the little individual desks. The Instructor, who appeared to me to be Merlin the Magician, came in and told me, "When you are ready, you can learn anything here." I thanked him and told him I will return after the end of the 40 days; he smiled and disappeared. The Learning Room, which I have also heard this 'place' called The Library, soon became my metaphor for the Universal Akashic Records, and it has now been incorporated into the ILC Meditation.

After visiting each of the four rooms in your Temple during your 40-Day Journey, you stop briefly at the altar and offer thanks for this experience. Then you exit through the Temple doors and prepare to return to your meadow. As you descend your spiritual mountain, you bring with you all the memories and energies of your Temple experience in the White Garden down into the Violet Garden and merge these energies. Then you will bring these merged energies down into the Blue Garden and merge them once again. In a similar fashion, you blend and merge all the energies of each chakra garden with all the others, balancing and harmonizing the energies of each chakra as you descend. This is a very important process and brings back into your physical awareness the memories, knowledge, insights and higher energies of your spiritual meditation.

As you cross your bridge and return to your meadow, you again sense the vitality and energy of all the life in your meadow and, when you are ready, gently step back into your Point of Perfect Balance in your meadow, and then into the Point of Perfect Balance within your physical self, bringing with you all the insights and knowledge of your meditation experience, as well as the healing energies of balance, renewal and regeneration.

After you have successfully made the 40 consecutive day meditation journey, you are well-prepared to delve deeper into the mysteries in each of the rooms in your Temple. Because you are going to be doing deeper work each time you visit one of your Temple rooms, you will need to spend more time in that room. Therefore, it is important to shorten the length of time spent in your overall meditation schedule.

The ILC Meditation contains a very powerful and effective set of spiritual tools that anyone can use to change the way they live their life and interact with others. But in order to make a difference, this meditation is best used regularly and purposefully. At this point, you must walk your own walk. Rev. Solomon and I have provided you these tools to let you explore your own consciousness and abilities, but we cannot do the exploration for you.

I sincerely thank Paul's widow, Sharon Solomon, and The Paul Solomon Foundation, for giving me their kind permission to use the material from Paul's workshops to record my own adaptation of his meditation on a CD in my own voice and to offer it to the public. Additional information about Rev. Solomon, his teachings and The Paul Solomon Foundation can be found at www.paulsolomon.com. If you are interested in also experiencing the ILC Meditation, I have provided a link on my website to freely download a self-extracting .zip file that contains the complete meditation and instruction manual for use of both the full "40-Day Mediation" and the shorter "ILC Meditation." On the Internet, go to www.howardbatie.com, click on the menu link for "ILC Meditation" and then click on the "Click Here to Download The ILC Meditation" link.

Focused Breathwork. One of the workshops I attended while in Virginia Beach, VA had as its objective to place me and the other workshop attendees into a higher state of conscious awareness through only a directed breathwork technique. Repeated rapid deep breathing did indeed cause an altered state of awareness, but I would characterize it more as hyperventilation without any spiritual benefits, and I came out of the experience quite dizzy and disoriented, not at all what I had been led to expect.

However, things always happen for a reason. Many years later, I was investigating possible techniques to coach my students into their Spiritual Area without the self-hypnosis required by the Spiritual Journeys technique described below. I revisited the focused breathwork process (but without the hyperventilation), coupled it with a guided visualization sequence provided by Archangel Michael as the Infinity

Breath, and incorporated the amazing Scalar Energy discoveries of the late Dr. Valerie Hunt (Professor Emeritus of Physiological Sciences at the University of California in Los Angeles) into a powerful, remote spiritual healing technique that could repeatedly produce verifiable physical or emotional results experienced by my (usually remote) clients. From the feedback received from my remote clients, I recognized that these positive results could be provided only if I had been in my Spiritual Area and was working with the spiritual energies available there. I documented this technique and called it "Trans-Scalar Healing." Details are in my 2017 book, *"Trans-Scalar Healing: Holistic Healing for Self, Others and Gaia."*

The sequence for effectively preparing yourself as an effective and proficient remote spiritual healer, as well as to train other facilitators to do the same, is herewith freely made available to the public and is taught in three-steps, as further discussed on my website: https://www.howardbatie.com.

Step 1 – Self Healing. View the 72-minute narrated PowerPoint Presentation "Intro To Trans-Scalar Healing 3.0" provided in the free download from my website; it is also available on YouTube (search for "Evergreen Healing Arts Center"). Using the procedures provided in the narrated PowerPoint Presentation, ground yourself, cleanse and balance your own chakras and meridians, connect to Universal Healing energies using Archangel Michael's "Infinity Breath" guided visualization, self-generate a powerful Scalar Energy field within your own physical body and energetic aura, and invoke highest dimensional Scalar healing energies to bring the highest possible healing energies to yourself first before you proceed to bring healing energies to another person.

Step 2 – Enter Your Spiritual Area. After establishing your self-healing Scalar Energy Field, you will be coached to raise your conscious awareness into the spiritual realms using the 26-minute .mp3 audio file that can be downloaded from the TSH page on my website (www.howardbatie.com); you will also be coached how to meet and consciously exchange information with your own Higher Self and Spirit Guide, learn how to call for and challenge your remote client's Higher Self, and how to banish any negative intruders or impostors.

Step 3 – Temple of Healing. You, the facilitator as your Higher Self, will provide a very effective energy healing session to your remote client's Higher Self using Scalar Energy or any other healing energy you are trained in (Reiki, Healing Touch, Qi Gong, Theta Healing, etc.), you will consciously dialogue and interact with the Healing Angels, and also bring higher-dimensional healing energies to the Collective Consciousness of Humanity and to Mother Earth.

While developing and refining the Trans-Scalar Healing processes, I have conducted both local healing sessions (the client was in my physical presence) and remote healing sessions (the client was not in my physical presence and could be anywhere in the world). The healing results were equally apparent in either case; however, I soon chose to concentrate solely on remote healing, since working with a client in my physical presence audibly and visually distracted me from the expanded state of awareness I felt was necessary for close interaction with the spiritual assistance available.

An additional benefit of working only remotely is that it ensures that the practitioner learns to trust their own intuitive ability to receive information from external sources, information that is personally relevant for their clients; further, this ability continues to be noticeably enhanced and reinforced with each remote spiritual healing session provided. As I have developed and practiced this technique, the only information I want to know about the client before the session is conducted is their full name and physical address at the time of the remote healing; this format of working "blind" to their physical, emotional and mental condition and symptoms requires me to rely solely on the information provided intuitively in my dialogues with my client's Higher Self and the Angelic assistants. The consistently positive results for the client and the continuing reinforcement of my own intuitive abilities have led me to discontinue all local client healing sessions and rely solely on this remote healing process as my preferred method for providing healing sessions.

I am no longer providing instructional workshops that teach this technique in person. However, I have made available all the materials that would teach a student to facilitate extremely effective remote spiritual healing sessions with direct Angelic assistance and support, as well as to provide complete training workshops to teach others how to do the same. The training materials include the Step 1 narrated PowerPoint presentation ("Intro To Trans-Scalar Healing 3 0") which is available from YouTube (search for "Evergreen Healing Arts Center"), and the Step 2 .mp3 audio file that can be freely downloaded from the TSH page on my website. This file will coach clients into their Spiritual Area. Complete detailed Step 3 instructions and dialog for the entire Trans-Scalar Healing program are provided in the step-by-step instruction manual which is available in either paperback book or Kindle format from Amazon.com; on Amazon, search for "Howard Batie" to view my publications.

Hypnotic Techniques. As a Certified Hypnotherapist and a long-standing member of the American Board of Hypnotherapy, the National Guild of Hypnotists, and the International Medical and Dental Hypnotherapy Association, I have met and exchanged information with many other Hypnotists and Hypnotherapists, and have learned much from their own experiences and teachings. The annual conventions of these and other organizations also provided many opportunities to attend lectures and experiential workshops on a wide variety of hypnotic techniques and processes such as pain management, stress and anxiety release, stop smoking, sports hypnosis, and many other topics, including one that I was particularly interested in – Spiritual Hypnosis. In addition, lecture notes, books and training manuals for many hypnotic applications were available at these annual conferences, at brick-and-mortar bookstores such as Barnes & Noble, as well as from on-line sources such as Amazon.com. There seemed to be a rapidly growing body of knowledge about things metaphysical, and I was eagerly exploring the spiritual experiences and techniques of others Hypnotherapists as much as I could.

The modalities and techniques discussed below are based on the use of hypnosis and can, therefore, be provided to interested clients only by a properly trained and experienced Hypnotherapist or Hypnotist.

Life Between Lives Hypnotherapy. In 2001, I attended the annual convention of The American Board of Hypnotherapy in San Diego, CA, where I provided a presentation on Ro-Hun Transformational Therapy, discussed above. While I was there, I also attended a lecture given by Dr. Michael Newton; he presented the results of his 35 years of experience as a traditionally-trained Clinical Psychologist investigating and cataloguing the spiritual experiences of his clients between their past lives using a technique he called Spiritual Regression (which later evolved into "Life Between Lives Hypnotherapy"). I immediately bought his books, *Journey of Souls* and *Destiny of Souls*, and focused my own hypnotherapy practice on further exploration of this hugely fascinating area. In 2005, I attended his workshop in Boulder, CO and took the training to become a Life Between Lives (LBL) Practitioner, and after providing and documenting several LBL sessions with my own clients, in 2006 I became fully certified as an LBL Practitioner.

My clients soon taught me that this realm we all exist in *between* physical incarnations is one of complete joy and freedom, healing, happiness, life review, contemplation and planning. It is in that realm that we prepare for our next (or current) physical lifetime under the wise guidance and mentoring of our Spirit Guide and a group of advanced souls collectively known as "The Council" or "The Council Of Elders" (see Chapter 2 for more information about Collective Consciousnesses).

The current LBL process has been based on the observations given to Dr. Newton by his clients over his professional 35-year career in over 7,000 spiritual regressions. As described in his books, "*Journey of Souls*" and "*Destiny of Souls*," after being gently and very deeply hypnotized to experience their most recent past lifetime, most of Dr. Newton's clients reviewed and described four distinct and separate areas of spiritual experience: (1) their "Gateway" experience where they meet a spiritual "Greeter" who escorts their energies Home after the death of their physical body. There, the negative memories and energies of a traumatic lifetime and/or death are removed and healed as appropriate by spiritual healers, they meet their Spirit Guide, and are escorted to their Soul Group for a joyous reunion; (2) they relax and participate in any enjoyable activity that they wish (e.g., dancing and singing, reading in the Library, exploring other worlds, learning to manipulate energy, etc.); (3) they meet with their Guide to plan their next (or current) physical incarnation, and also meet with their Council of Elders who provide any final recommendations for the upcoming life plan, and (4) go to the Incarnation Room where they preview a range of possible physical bodies, and choose the specific body and family that will best allow them to learn and grow from the lessons they have chosen to learn in their next (or current) physical lifetime.

To carry on his remarkable and award-winning ground-breaking work in the field of metaphysics, Dr. Newton founded "The Newton Institute (TNI) for Life Between Lives (LBL) Hypnotherapy," and under the skillful guidance of its first President, Paul Aurand of the USA, and his successor Peter Smith of Australia, TNI has steadily grown and expanded its reach world-wide. In response to the growing interest in and demand for personal experience of the spiritual realms, as of June 2018, LBL Hypnotherapy sessions are being provided in over 40 countries and in 20 different languages by a worldwide and steadily growing network of over 220 trained LBL Hypnotherapists. Two trainings to become an LBL Hypnotherapist are normally held each year, one in the USA and one in another country, and are conducted only by fully trained and TNI-Certified Instructors. These classes are extended only to certified Hypnotherapists who have been properly trained and credentialed by a recognized Hypnosis training school. In addition, prospective students must submit documentation of extensive experience conducting both in-utero and past life regression sessions, and they must also agree to abide by the strict Code of Ethics established by TNI. See their website (www.newtoninstitute.org) for further details and to locate the nearest LBL practitioner to you.

Any further description by me of this wonderful technique would not begin to do justice to the wealth of information provided in Dr. Newton's ground-breaking books (see Bibliography), and the reader is encouraged to review this new map of the spiritual experiences provided by his several thousand LBL sessions. Additional information about this remarkable technique is also available on the Facebook page for The Newton Institute.

Ultra-Height. One of the most highly recognized practitioners in the field of Hypnosis was the late Gerald ("Jerry") Kein, who shared his experience and knowledge in many areas of hypnotic specialization, including several metaphysical applications such as Past Life Regression, Spiritual Regression, and a unique technique he called Ultra-Height. He developed, practiced and taught Ultra-Height, but only to other spiritually-oriented Hypnotherapists, as a technique to allow the Hypnotherapist to talk directly with the hypnotized client's 'Inner Wisdom,' or as I call it, their Higher Self. His theory was that each person's Higher Self has all the answers to every emotional situation or physical condition or disease that is not medically responsive – how, when and why it was created – and that the Higher Self must be consulted to ensure that releasing the condition or 'curing' the disease would be in the highest and best interests of the soul. The overall process summarized below is a condensed summary of Mr. Kein's Ultra-Height technique.

The hypnotic process begins by placing the client into a very deep state of hypnosis, even deeper than the traditional state of physical and mental relaxation called Somnambulism, into the deep hypnotic Esdaile state characterized by very slow brain wave activity of the lower Theta region (4-7 cycles per second). The deeply hypnotized client would then be coached 'up' into an expanded state of awareness by successively and slowly counting the client 'up' from 1 to 10 four or five times in a row, allowing the client's awareness to move 'higher' and expand more and more with each 1-to-10 counting sequence until they become aware of the presence of their Inner Wisdom or similar metaphor for their Higher Self.

When the client's Higher Self is recognized, the client is asked to describe what it is that they want to release, and a dialog is begun between the Hypnotherapist and the client's Higher Self to determine if the client's own inner resources are aware of how that limiting condition or disease was created. If so, the conversation then explores how that limitation is negatively affecting them in their current lifetime. The dialog with the client's Higher Self then continues with asking if it would be in their highest and best good to release or eliminate the limitation; only the Higher Self would have that information. The client's Higher Self is then asked if it is able to release the condition by itself. If not, bring in the Angelic healers to assist. If so, the Higher Self is then directed to release the limitation, as well as all memory of the limitation, and is given a period of time to do that. When the process is complete, the client is emerged from hypnosis and asked to compare how their entire energy system 'feels' compared that to how they felt before.

It is important that this Ultra-Height technique be provided by an experienced Hypnotherapist; the above abbreviated overview of this very powerful technique is a best-case scenario that works as described "at least fifty to sixty percent of the time," according to a personal conversation I had with Mr. Kein at one of the National Guild of Hypnotists annual conventions we both attended. I have adapted his process to improve its reliability for consistently accessing the expanded awareness of the Spiritual Area, and have incorporated these adaptations into the Spiritual Journeys process discussed below.

Spiritual Journeys. Spiritual Journeys is a self-hypnosis program that is taught and practiced by a Certified

Hypnotherapist; Spiritual Journeys session can teach any interested client: First, how to bring themselves into a state of deep self-hypnosis whenever they want to, and all by themselves; Secondly, to then raise their conscious awareness into their Spiritual Area; and, Thirdly, to consciously meet and converse with their own Higher Self and Spirit Guide. In my Hypnotherapy practice, I have found that these three objectives are most effectively accomplished when each step is provided in separate hypnosis sessions about one week apart, allowing the client to practice each step before proceeding to the next step. These three sessions provide the necessary foundation for all future Spiritual Journeys you may wish to take, and are discussed below; several additional and optional Journeys to begin exploring the infinitely vast spiritual realms are described in the following section, "Exploring Your Expanded Awareness." A complete overview of the Spiritual Journeys program is provided in my book, "*Spiritual Journeys: A Practical Methodology for Accelerated Spiritual Development and Experiential Exploration.*"

Session 1 - Self-Hypnosis. The first Spiritual Journeys session usually takes about 3 hours and begins with an informational interview, called a "Pre-Talk," to discuss the client's personal objectives, to inform them about What Hypnosis Is and Isn't, and to determine how they best process information, whether that is Visually, Aurally or Kinesthetically. This determination is simple to make and is particularly important; for example, if the client is not primarily Visual, they would not be asked in deep hypnosis to "see" the tree; instead they would be ask you to "become aware of the tree" without specifying what sense to use. It is also important to emphasize that the Hypnotherapist cannot make the client do anything they do not want to do or is not safe for them; furthermore, they will not even allow themselves to become very deeply hypnotized unless they completely trust their

Hypnotherapist. Therefore, the Hypnotherapist will first need to allay all of the client's fears and misconceptions about hypnosis and earn that trust.

When the Hypnotherapist and client have a strong degree of trust between them, the client will be asked to rest comfortably in "the most comfortable recliner in THIS galaxy" and the Hypnotherapist will provide to the client those instruction that will relax them physically and mentally, going deeper and deeper relaxed only when they are ready and want to enjoy a deeper state of relaxation. When they are completely relaxed physically and mentally in very deep hypnosis, they will then be given the instructions to follow each time when they are completely conscious and awake, and want to return to this comfortable and safe feeling of very deepest relaxation that they are able to enjoy... today.

These instructions include two increments; the First is for them to state out loud their clear intentions, and the Second is to raise and drop their Index Finger. The instant they FEEL their finger touching whatever it is resting on, they instantly return to the deepest level of self-hypnosis they are able to feel... today. The Hypnotherapist will then instruct the hypnotized client on how to quickly and easily emerge themselves from self-hypnosis and return to full conscious awareness. Then the hypnotized client will be asked to emerge themselves back to full conscious awareness, and will practice returning to deep self-hypnosis several times by themselves; this will allow them to build confidence in their ability to do this all by themselves any time they wish. The client will then be given a Deepening CD that is to be used at least once a day for about a week or more; each time the Deepening CD is played, it will move the client into an even deeper state of relaxation.

Session 2 - Accessing The Spiritual Area. The second Spiritual Journeys session begins by asking the client to get comfortable in that recliner again, set their intentions out loud, raise and drop their Index Finger and move into deep self-hypnosis. Within a few seconds, they are very deeply self-hypnotized and ready to receive additional instructions on how to safely expand their awareness into their Spiritual Area.

The first step is to determine if the client really is ready to move into their Spiritual Area where there is only light and love, happiness and joy. They will be instructed to create a wonderful, protective cocoon of safety and love around their physical body and conscious mind, and when they confirm the feelings of both safety and love, they are ready to take the next step. In my experience, ninety-nine percent of my students have been ready, but a few were not – they were unable to feel the love surrounding them, and it is only that feeling of safety and love that allows them to let that other part of mind – the higher mind, Inner Wisdom, Higher Self, or whatever you want to call it – to lift and rise through the cocoon and continue on its way toward their Spiritual Area. In each case when a block prevented them from feeling love, conducting a separate hypnotic regression session to determine and release the cause of the block allowed the client to then return to the Spiritual Journeys process and successfully continue their journey 'upward' toward their Spiritual Area.

When the client feels both safety and love, they are coached to 'rise higher' into an Emotional level of awareness where there is only love, light, happiness, joy and compassion. When they feel that love and joy, they are then instructed to bring that love and light with them as they are coached even higher into another Mental level where all the ideas and beliefs that are held as true are surrounded and blended with the love and light that was also brought forward. They are then coached to move even higher, even beyond the need for information into an infinite <u>Spiritual</u> level where they can just BE and rest for a moment. By bringing their awareness up from the physical body, which continues to safely rest in the cocoon below, up through their Emotional and Mental Selves and into their Spiritual Higher Self's consciousness, they have lifted their awareness up through their entire energy system and into their own experience of their Spiritual Area. They are then instructed to repeat out loud a short prayer: "Dear Creator, I ask that your Light and Love surround and protect me always." Interestingly, in the deepest levels of hypnosis, the client is unable to speak at all, but after rising into their Spiritual Area, they can easily use their voice to speak very clearly.

The client is then given the instructions that teach them how to return from this expanded state of awareness to full conscious awareness; after this is practiced several times, they are given another audio CD that coaches them to move into deep self-hypnosis and to then rise into their Spiritual Area using the techniques they have been taught. They are asked to practice with the CD each day for about a week before returning for their third Spiritual Journeys session.

Session 3 - Meeting Higher Self & Spirit Guide. During the client's third Spiritual Journeys session, they are asked to get comfortable in the recliner and move into their Spiritual Area using the technique they have been taught, and to then let the Hypnotherapist know when they are there just by saying "OK" or "I'm here" out loud. Less than a minute later, they are usually ready and, from the awareness of their Higher Self, say "OK." The client is then taught how to set their intentions to work in the spiritual realms. Immediately upon entering your Spiritual Area, they must make sure that they do the three simple but necessary things that must always be done each time they come to their Spiritual Area: (1) call for

Creator's light and love to surround and protect them always; (2) establish a clear channel of communication between themselves and the highest levels of Love and Wisdom; and (3) state their intention that all information they receive be only for the greater good of all concerned. This can easily include the initial short prayer provided above, and be combined into a single statement of intention by saying out loud:

Dear Creator, I ask that your Light and Love surround and protect me always. I ask that a clear and open channel of communication be established NOW between me and the highest levels of love and wisdom, and that all information I receive be for the Greater Good of all concerned. Thank You!

It is important that the word NOW be included in the request for establishment of a clear channel of communication. When the client is in their Spiritual Area, their awareness will be operating in the 5th Dimension of consciousness where there is no past or future "time;" there is only the present "NOW."

Once the client has risen into their Spiritual Area, their awareness is that of their own Higher Self, and one of the first things they will do is to become aware of how they appear to others in the spiritual world. They will be introduced to their "spiritual mirror" that reflects how they appear to other spiritual beings here in their Spiritual Area. It could be like looking in the bathroom mirror at home, or it could be as a shining ball of pulsing energy, or anything in between, but they will <u>know</u> that they are seeing themselves, and will be asked to indelibly record this image and feeling in their eternal spiritual memory.

Next, the client is taught how to call forward and challenge any other spiritual being they may meet, beginning with their own

Spirit Guide. When they know or sense that they are protected, they are instructed to call their Spirit Guide forward in a form they can recognize by saying out loud:

I call on my Spirit Guide to come forward in a form that I can recognize.

If specific information is provided about the appearance of their Spirit Guide – their stance, the way they move, or their personality, etc., this additional information can be jotted down in a note with the details so it can be recorded for future reference. The client may also be coached to ask this being what name they wish to be called – what their name or vibration would sound like if it could be spoken in the higher realms. Simply asking, "What is your name?" would be improper because spirit beings don't have "names;" instead, they are known in the spirit realms by the energetic and vibrational frequencies that they radiate. Simply ask the spiritual being:

What name would you like me to call you?

Alternatively, a similar invitation can be extended to any spirit being that the client wishes to speak with. For instance, if they wish to call forward Archangel Raphael and discuss a topic with him, they could say:

I invite Archangel Raphael to come forward now and present yourself in a form that I can recognize.

Or, if the practitioner is preparing to offer a remote healing session, for example, for Sally Smith in Akron, OH, they could call for Sally's Higher Self to come forward and be recognized:

89

I call on the Higher Self of Sally Smith at 123 Anywhere Street in Akron, Ohio, to come forward and present yourself in a form that I can recognize.

Many times, the street address isn't necessary, but can always be included, since there may be several Sally Smiths in Akron, Ohio.

Challenge And Banishment. When any being is called forward, the client must also be prepared to occasionally encounter spirit beings who are still learning the benefits of cooperation instead of competition (Service to Others vs. Service to Self); therefore, it is essential that the client know how to positively identify the being that comes forward and how to banish any intruder or deceiver. After the client has called a being forward, the client will observe who or what appears before them. It may look like the intended being, or perhaps it may look like an animal totem, a symbol, or other energy form that represents the being called forward. The client must always make sure that they confirm first, that the being called forward is working with the forces of Light, and secondly, that they are actually the being called forward. For instance, if a being called forward appears like a farmer in bib overalls, the first step of this process is to simply challenge the being:

Farmer, are you in service to the Light and Love of the One Infinite Creator - Yes or No?

No other alternatives for an answer are permitted, and do not be concerned about challenging even an Archangel; any being of Light will honor your request without being offended. However, Intruders, Tricksters or Dark Entities cannot say Yes to the challenge. If the one being challenged does not immediately repeat back the answer "Yes" without any hedging or hesitation, it can be assumed that they are NOT who was invited to come forward. In this case, the intruder must be banished from your presence by saying out loud:

Farmer, In the Name of the One Infinite Creator, I COMMAND you to leave my presence immediately and permanently. So be it!

When anything is commanded of a being in the Name of the Creator, they being must, and do, obey. Then another invitation for the intended spirit being to come forward may be issued and the challenge repeated. If the challenge is readily answered with a Yes, the being has confirmed that they are working with the forces of Light, not Darkness, and the next task is to ensure that they are in fact who was called forward:

Are you in fact Archangel Raphael (or the Higher Self of Sally Smith with whom I am to work today) – Yes or No?

If this being says No, you have already determined that they are working with the Light, so ask why they have come to you today, and receive the information they have for you. Then release them and call again for the one you wish to speak with, and again challenge whoever appears. To release them, say out loud:

Thank you for coming today and sharing that information. You are released to go about your own activities.

If they say Yes - they are the being you called forward - ask them to approach closer and look into their eyes if they have eyes, feel their energies, and trust what you feel.

Without exception, every single being that is encountered in the Spiritual Area must be challenged and confirmed, even if it is a being that has been met and challenged many times before. Don't worry about offending spirit beings by challenging them – the good ones sincerely appreciate the fact that you are very discerning about whom you allow into your presence. Just be aware that in the higher realms, many higher dimensional beings can assume the shape or form of anyone or anything, including a being you have met before.

Using the spiritual name provided makes it easier for the hypnotized client to maintain the proper state of mental relaxation throughout the hypnotic session. Also, if, during a local healing session, your client's Higher Self has presented itself in a form other than human (animal, totem, ball of light, etc.), it is perfectly permissible to ask them to assume a human form similar to a physical body so it will be easier to work with them during the healing that you will provide later. You could say:

(Being, object, symbol, etc.), please assume a human form that will be easier for me to work with. Thank you.

Record the form they morphed from and also the form morphed into so you can discuss the potential meaning with the client later if you wish.

The Two-Way Dialog. Once the client has confirmed that they are in the presence of their Spirit Guide, they are also taught how to begin conversing in a conscious two-way dialog with their Guide. Each person's Higher Self and Spirit Guide are excellent sources of helpful information and guidance to ease their journey through each day's obstacles and challenges. Initially, before they enter their Spiritual Area, the client is asked to write down a single short question that they would like answered, and when they do that, they are instructed to forget about the question altogether. Later, when

92

the self-hypnotized client is in the presence of, for example, their Guide, they will open their eyes and read the question aloud, and then quickly close their eyes again and listen for the answer from their Guide. When they read the question, they don't have to 'think' about the question, and can remain in an expanded state of awareness while they listen to the Guide 'speak'. It also helps to have a digital voice recorder handy so they can record the verbally spoken information provided by the Guide. During subsequent journeys to their Spiritual Area, the client can ask two questions, and steadily begin to consciously interact more conversationally with their Guide.

Upon completion of this third Spiritual Journeys session, the client has established a solid foundation for easily gaining a higher perspective from the information provided by their spiritual mentors; in addition, they are well-prepared to begin safely exploring the spiritual realms.

Exploring Your Expanded Awareness

Once the client is in the expanded conscious awareness in their Spiritual Area, regardless of the technique used to get there, their Higher Self's awareness is then free to explore all the information available in the spiritual realms, as well as their own innate spiritual abilities, if they wish. While constructing the Spiritual Journeys program, three optional avenues of investigation have been identified, if the client wishes to continue and explore further: First, the natural ability of each person to bring healing energies to themselves and others; Second, the nature of their personal spiritual essence and history; and Third, any information in the Universal Akashic Records.

As it is now constructed, the Spiritual Journeys program is the specific modality I settled on that would easily allow my clients to become aware of, and actually experience, their own spiritual abilities. When I began to explore the unlimited information in the spirit realms, the first area of interest to me was that of spiritual healing, the metaphysical ability that I was first introduced to after I listened to 'The Voice' and began my own Journey. You may also wish to explore this and/or other areas that are interesting and important for you personally; instead of spiritual healing, you might want to investigate architecture, music, philosophy, technology, cultural characteristics of various civilizations, or any other topic at all. They are all now available for humans to investigate, learn and grow.

Spiritual Healing. It may not initially be obvious how the subject of Spiritual Healing would contribute to the subject of Metaphysical Communication, the primary objective of this book. However, I have found through my own experience as both an energy healing facilitator and as a Hypnotherapist that, when practiced regularly, energy healing techniques do contribute strongly to the development of one's intuitive senses; synergistically, when one is receiving intuitive information about what the body may need energetically, there is a powerful feedback communication on how to proceed for the client's greatest good and most beneficial use of the healing energies. Therefore, I believe that any process that strengthens the development of one's inner senses – including meditation, guided visualization, energy healing, etc. – will also open the lines of communication with one's higher resources and lead to expansion of conscious awareness.

One of the tenets of most introductory energy healing workshops (Reiki, Healing With Color & Sound, Healing Touch, etc.) is that it is important for the practitioner to heal themselves first, before attempting to bring healing energies to another person. If this is not done prior to a healing session, the healing practitioner will be bringing the energy of their own negative feelings, emotions, biases, prejudices, and limitations to the healing session. The healing practitioner will need to clear these limitations and blockages within their own energy field (aura) before interacting with someone else's energy field, and to do otherwise would not be in the best interests of either the practitioner or the client. Once the negative energies are released from the practitioner's energy field (energy chakras, energy meridians, and energy bodies), only then will they be best able to facilitate a healing session that is most beneficial for the client; only then will they become the best possible instrument of healing that they can be to assist in returning the client to a higher state of health and wellness on all levels of their being.

There are several ways an energy field may be cleared of obstructions, distortions and limitations, and I have fully documented the method I prefer in my book *"Trans-Scalar Healing: Holistic Healing For Self, Others and Gaia"*. The reason I prefer it is because, if done conscientiously, it completely clears and balances all three components of the practitioner's electromagnetic energy field: the seven primary chakras plus the Ascension Chakra external to the physical body, all primary energy meridians associated with the Traditional Chinese Medicine technique of Acupuncture, as well as all five concentric energy bodies (physical, etheric, emotional, mental and spiritual) that make up the human energetic Aura. Nothing external to the practitioner (e.g., objects, crystals, smudging, etc.) is required, and only a specific breathing process and focused intention are all that you need.

Self-Healing. Once the three components of the practitioner's energy field are cleared and balanced, the practitioner is well prepared to act as an instrument of healing for themselves or for their clients, whether the client is in the practitioner's physical presence or anywhere in the world. The old adage "Physician, heal thyself <u>first</u>!" is quite appropriate, and should always be observed as the first step when intending to bring healing energies to anyone. The practitioner may connect with and invoke the healing energies of any technique that they have been taught, such as Reiki, Healing Touch, Qi Gong, Theta Healing, etc. If they have not been trained in any such energy healing technique, the quantum Scalar Energies of the Bio-Scalar Healing Technique, taught by the late Dr. Valerie Hunt, may be invoked. These procedures for creating a healing Scalar Energy field around you with a non-hypnotic breathing process are also included and fully described in the book *Trans-Scalar Healing* mentioned above. Once Scalar Energies have been created within the practitioner's energetic aura, a powerful Self-Healing Decree can then be issued out loud to clear their own energy field and for self-healing of the practitioner.

The Trans-Scalar Healing process, although extremely effective in its own right, is not the only beneficial Self-Healing technique. The guided visualization and imagery provided by the Inner Light Consciousness Meditation's Healing Room in the temple at the top of the mountain is another avenue to bring self-healing energies to the practitioner.

In the ILC Meditation's Healing Room, the practitioner is guided to meet Archangel Raphael, the Archangel of Healing, and rest comfortably on the Healing Table in the center of the room. There, Raphael and his Healing Angels will, upon your request, provide a healing experience to restore your entire energetic being to the highest level and degree of health and wellness that is appropriate at that time, consistent with the practitioner's own soul contracts and chosen Life Purpose. When the practitioner is informed, or just knows that additional healing energies are no longer required, they will thank

Archangel Raphael, the Angels, and Creator, and be escorted back down the mountain again, bringing with them the healing energies and the conscious memory of this experience. When they re-enter their Meadow, they will integrate the entire experience back into their physical body and conscious mind, and then return full mental awareness to continue their day.

Healing Others. The Healing Room in the ILC Meditation Room was developed primarily as a place where the practitioner can bring healing energies to themselves; however, in the Spiritual Journeys program, the Healing Room has been adapted to bring the same healing energies to anyone the practitioner chooses. A significant difference is that the ILC Meditation uses guided visualization to move the practitioner into their Healing Room in their Spiritual Area, while the initial Spiritual Journeys healing session (Spiritual Journey #4) is based on self-hypnosis to accomplish the same goal. It doesn't really matter how the practitioner moves into their Spiritual Area, but once there, the healing process is basically the same: turn the actual spiritual healing efforts over to Archangel Raphael and his Healing Angels. Nevertheless, important experience will have been gained by the practitioner while working in the higher energies of their own Higher Self and the Angelic Kingdom.

The next level of spiritual healing proficiency is to perform the actual energetic spiritual healing process yourself instead of relying on Archangel Raphael and the Healing Angels. In Spiritual Journey #5, the healing practitioner will be the one actually conducting the entire spiritual healing session with the assistance of the Healing Angels; in order to do this, the practitioner will consciously establish a two-way dialog with the Healing Angels, who will offer only the assistance asked for by the practitioner. Once in their Spiritual Area, the practitioner will call for the Higher Self of their client to come forward, properly challenge them, and ask the client's Higher Self if they would like to accompany the practitioner to their Temple of Healing; in my experience, no Higher Self has ever declined this invitation. Consent by the client's Higher Self to accompany the practitioner to the Temple of Healing is all the permission needed; and consciously asking for permission is not necessary, since the conscious mind really knows only what it wants, not what is in its Higher Self's greater good.

The remainder of the healing session is identical to the Trans-Scalar Healing process discussed in detail in my 2017 book, "*Trans-Scalar Healing.*" With the client's Higher Self resting on the comfortable Healing Table, several nets of golden light are drawn through their energy field. With these nets, the practitioner successively locates and removes any negative attached entities, any invited entities in their aura, any negative object or implants left behind by someone else, and any negative or limiting thoughtforms that might inhibit their physical, emotional, mental or spiritual growth and evolution. After each pass of the nets, a conversation is begun with the Angels to discuss and confirm or modify what the practitioner has intuitively captured or felt as the net passed through the energy field of the client's Higher Self. This is the perfect blend of both Spiritual Healing and Metaphysical Communication.

Once all negative, limiting, 'not-client' energies have been removed, the practitioner directs the Angels to move out into all the dimensions to locate and, in a process similar to shamanic soul retrieval, to return any of the client's own energies that may have been lost. These retrieved energies are then re-integrated back into the client's energy field, making them energetically whole and complete once more with all of their own energies and no negative energies from someone else. This is the point at which any positive or healing energies will be most effective and beneficial, since there will be no negative energies remaining in the client's energy field that might distort or deflect the healing energies.

The practitioner will then ask the Angels to identify the most beneficial healing technique that they have been trained in (the Angels always know your own energies!), and then connect with and provide those healing energies to the client on the table. In my experience, 99% of the time the Angels have identified Reiki as the most beneficial healing energy for the client at that time, although I am trained in several other energy healing techniques as well. And even if the practitioner is not trained in ANY healing technique other than Trans-Scalar Healing, the Scalar self-healing energies developed during the earlier practitioner preparation steps can be provided to the client's Higher Self. The practitioner can then step up to the Healing Table and provide a complete healing session, just as if the client was in the practitioner's physical presence. In the higher dimensions of mind, there is no Space and no Time, so you might find that only a few minutes of Earth time are required.

When the practitioner becomes aware that the flow of healing energy begins to subside a bit, the practitioner will issue the Healing Decree in the Name of the One Infinite Creator, and the then witness the healing. If there is any change in the appearance or actions of the client's Higher Self on the table, that can be taken as confirmation that the healing energies have been accepted, and that the healing will be completed by the physical client at the appropriate time. However, if no change is noticed by the practitioner, this would be an indication that some or all of the healing energies were not accepted by the client's Higher Self, and that the healing would not be as complete as consciously desired. Remember, the practitioner's role and responsibility is only to bring the healing energies to the client's Higher Self; however, the client is responsible for accepting the healing energies on a soul level for the healing energies to manifest in increased physical health and wellness.

Following the healing sequence, the practitioner will ask the client's Higher Self if they would like to assist in a special Planetary Healing Process; again, in my experience, the invitation has always been accepted. The practitioner and the client's Higher Self will then jointly ask that another channel of highest dimensional healing energy of the Violet Flame of Transmutation be established and brought down from Source to the Collective Consciousness of Humanity and deep into the core of Mother Earth. This allows healing energies to flow continuously to every living being on and in Mother Earth, and also enlists the help and assistance of Ascended Master St. Germain and Ascended Lady Master Kwan Yin, the guardians and directors of the energy of the Violet Flame of Transmutation.

After this powerful healing technique has been conducted several times and the practitioner has begun to receive positive feedback from their remote clients, they practitioner will have taken a huge step forward in trusting both the healing process and themselves as an instrument of that process. The practitioner is then ready to take the final step in the technique as it is presently constructed: working without any foreknowledge of what their client's condition is, or even what they might desire to have happen as a result of the healing session. This is where the practitioner takes a big leap of faith in themselves as a spiritual/energetic practitioner, as well as completely trusting the intuitive guidance received from their sources, whether those are the client's Higher Self, your own Higher Self, spirit Guides, Angelic Healers or other external sources who are always there to support and guide you. As always, the practitioner will learn the most about themselves and their own abilities when stretched beyond what they think is comfortable and what they think they are able to do. When working completely blinded to the remote client's medical and emotional condition and desires, and trusting the information that is being offered intuitively, the practitioner has indeed stepped into their own Mastery as a spiritual healing facilitator and can assist in manifesting whatever is most beneficial for their client at that time.

This Trans-Scalar Healing technique has become my primary tool for conducting remote healings on all levels for my clients for three very important reasons: First, from the unsolicited testimonials received from my clients, it is remarkably effective in addressing the client's needs on the physical, emotional, mental and spiritual levels; Second, a non-hypnotic technique is used to expand your awareness and access your Spiritual Area; and Third, this technique can be done by one person (the practitioner) anywhere, anytime and without a physical office setting, crystals, oils, essences, special lights or other objects. All that is required is a trained mind and a loving heart.

For a detailed step-by-step instruction manual and further information about this remarkable spiritual healing and angelic communication technique, see my 2017 book, *Trans-Scalar Healing: Holistic Healing For Self, Others and Gaia.*

Personal Spiritual Growth. The second optional pathway for exploring the spiritual realms using the Spiritual Journeys Program is for the client, under the direction of a trained Spiritual Journeys Teacher, to recall several significant experiences in their own soul's evolution and growth as a purely spiritual (non-physical) entity. Each person's own eternal soul record contains all the information and knowledge about everything that has been learned in all the experiences in all its travels throughout the cosmos since its creation by

Creator. Under the guidance and direction of an experienced Hypnotherapist, in four separate sessions, the client will take themselves into their Spiritual Area, and then vividly review and experience successively earlier spiritual experiences that are recorded in their Personal Akashic Record. In these four separate sessions, the client will review and re-live a pleasant non-therapeutic past lifetime on Earth, their very first lifetime on Planet Earth, their very first reactions and feelings of being an independent spiritual consciousness within the Universe, and their initial feelings and awareness at the instant of their soul's creation while still within and a part of the consciousness of Creator.

For each of these four Spiritual Journeys sessions, the client will be asked to rest comfortably in the recliner, to set their intentions to move into their Spiritual Area without a time limit, and do the three things they must always do when entering their Spiritual Area. In their Spiritual Area, they are consciously aware in an expanded state of consciousness, and are able to verbally channel what their Higher Self (soul essence) is aware of. The Director will then guide them to recall from their eternal soul memory the individual spiritual experience for that session, and the verbal information spoken will normally be recorded for their future review after returning to full conscious awareness.

The detailed transcripts from at least two separate case studies with different channels and clients for each of the four sessions in this pathway are provided in my 2015 book, "*Spiritual Journeys.*"

Pleasant Earth Past Lifetime. For those who have not had a Past Life Regression (PLR), this is a wonderful and gentle introduction into the vast storehouse of their own memories and experiences while incarnated on Earth. In this

PLR, we are not looking for any therapeutic outcome, not seeking to heal emotional wounds, and not searching for the cause of any traumatic physical or emotional issue; instead, it is a comfortable introduction that allows the client to become familiar with the process of retrieving and describing a pleasant life from another time, another place, another You. It could be a hundred years ago, or a thousand years ago; it could be in the country where they live today, or literally anywhere in the world; it could be as a man or as a woman (we have all been both), rich or poor, famous or common, with white or brown or black skin. The purpose here is to introduce the client gradually and comfortably into an earlier lifetime where they just know that it really is themselves in that lifetime, and to allow them to become comfortable with easily recalling memories and details that they could not have known consciously.

First Earth Lifetime. At some point in their soul's journey through this Universe, the client became aware of the existence of Planet Earth and chose to explore the energies and lessons of this world through a physical incarnation. So, where and when did a portion of their soul's energy (their Higher Self) first energetically merge with a physical body for an entire lifetime on Earth? Was it in a jungle, on a desert, a mountain, or a lowland by a sea or ocean? Were they a lonely nomad, or a member of a group of similar beings? What was their specific job or function within their group or clan? How was food prepared, and what did they eat? What kind of tools did they use? At the end of that first physical lifetime on Earth, what did they learn and how did they feel about that lifetime? Every person's experience is unique and fascinating, and the details that are consciously recalled from their spiritual memory will illuminate new and interesting facets of their life journey on Planet Earth.

First Independent Experience. Each individual's own Personal Akashic Record has within it all the memories, feelings, and experiences of their entire existence, including the moment their soul was liberated into the universe as an individual spiritual consciousness. During this Journey, the client will be guided to recall the very first memories, feelings and impressions at the moment of realization that their awareness was as an individual and independent spirit being within the Universe. Some of the interesting information that may be recalled includes: What did they FEEL at that moment? What were they aware of? What capabilities and characteristics did they have? What soul purpose did they choose – helper, explorer, healer, etc.? Who was there with them to help show the way? Where did they choose to go after being created, and why did they choose to go there?

This is a unique opportunity to dig even deeper into one's own soul purpose, and to learn how this dimension of pure consciousness was initially explored. Additionally, open-ended questioning such as "What did you choose to do then?" and "Where did you go next?" have led to many unexpected and interesting experiences, including visiting or incarnating on planets and worlds other than Earth, exploring non-physical worlds of sentient beings, and visiting and comparing the characteristics of other universes. This is also where the "young soul" may begin to learn about other worlds and universes they might have visited or incarnated into for lifetimes as a physical being or even as a non-corporeal (energetic, gaseous, etc.) life form.

Memories of Oneness. As the exploring client becomes more familiar with recovering information from their Personal Akashic Record, they may also wish to investigate their earliest experiences as a unique individual consciousness while still within the energy of Creator. These initial Memories

104

of Oneness with Creator are also recorded in the client's Personal Akashic Record and are available for recall as long as the client is ready for and can understand the meaning of the experience, it will be in the best interests of the individual to have that experience, and it will cause no harm to any living being. Among the many lines of inquiry that can be followed are: At the instant they were created and are still within the energy of the Creator – what were they aware of? What do they feel? What is Creator aware of? Does Creator have any thoughts? What does Creator feel? At that instant, did they know why they were created and what they were supposed to do?

Following these and other lines of inquiry that will come up during these Journeys can bring to light much knowledge about your true spiritual nature, your spiritual characteristics and abilities, and about the spiritual realms our Souls all live and play in. During the recollection of personal experiences in this Memories of Oneness Journey, it is usually better to have the information obtained from the Universal Akashic Record by your Guide rather than by your own Higher Self's awareness. Nearly all clients who have Journeyed this far have found that their Spirit Guide was present during the creation of their soul (their individual spiritual consciousness), but there have also been some for whom the client's Guide needed to step in and provide additional details to understand the experience with greater clarity.

Exploring The Universal Akashic Records. The third optional pathway for exploration of the spiritual realms is to examine the contents of the Universal Akashic Record. The initial exploration of this are began with an investigation into the nature, structure and composition of the Akashic Records themselves. Fortunately, the spiritual beings with whom we were communicating were very patient, and they explained that the Cosmic Akashic Record did have a structure to it that our human linear minds could understand – that of a single book that could be opened to a separate Chapter for each Universe, a sub-chapter for each Galaxy, a sub-heading for each Solar System, a paragraph for each world, and a sentence for each sentient being who had lived on that world either in physical or non-corporeal form. Further, when permission to access the Akashic Record was specifically requested and given, the spoken words "Akashic Record" acted as the password that allowed access to the specific information requested, and the locating of that information was done automatically, again with the three caveats discussed before. When one of the Channels in our Spiritual Research Group was asked to describe the information in their Personal Akashic Record, their response was:

The Personal Akashic Record contains the full developmental experience of an individual soul. It is a way to embody a soul's complete experience so that it might be not lost, so that it might be used, maintained, to have structure so that others can gain that information and for helping humanity's beings to move beyond the limits of their conscious awareness. The personal Akashic Record of Earth is the full developmental experience of the consciousness you call Gaia. The Galaxy also has a separate Akashic Record, as does this Universe, and the Universal Akashic Record is the memory of all that is, and that has been created by, the One Infinite Creator. Please understand the limitations of language here, because there is great power, knowledge and expansiveness beyond these words that cannot be conveyed. As you have many fingers on a hand, the One That Is All has many appendages of consciousness, and Its nature is to grow, and so it determines when something is needed to help the growth. And at one point in this part of your Milky Way Galaxy it was determined that it was time for individual consciousnesses to learn to associate and grow together, and so a planet was needed that would help them, over generations, learn to come together to work on a project and create life that blends, that becomes an amalgam. At that time of cosmic influences, the form of Earth was created and in the beginning was imbued with the consciousness you call Gaia. So, we have a separate level of Akashic Records for individuals, planets, Solar Systems, for Galaxies, but the One That Is All __is__ the Akashic Record in a more defined form in the sense that the One That Is All knows all that has happened; therefore, when it is appropriate, the Akashic Record is a term that is used here for asking for that kind of information from the One That Is All. It is the One That Is All who knows all that has been. In the human experience, the term "Akashic Record" is used as a password to gain access to that information and then you say, "Akashic Record, I need...." Access to information from the One That Is All is always done in a form suitable to those who are asking. We have brought you this client because her mind and her essence go beyond definition and structures, and she is able to comprehend the extension, the wholeness of something. And she understands that it is only the human mind and its language that creates these definitions to make it possible to speak of them. So, as you form your questions and begin to do more of your work, it might help if you keep in mind that you are using a false definition in the sense that it is only used this way on Earth, and that other universes, other planets, other beings have a different way of asking what you are asking, of trying to go beyond the limits of their consciousness. Do you understand?

The scope of the information available in the Cosmic Akashic Record is infinite and encompasses all the experiences, beings, deeds, thoughts and ideas contained in the Universal Akashic Record of each of the infinite number of universes. Our Spiritual Research Group continues to investigate the several realms of existence within our own universe, such as the Angelic Realm (Elohim, Angels and Archangels, etc.), the Spiritual Realms (Ascended Masters, evolved corporeal and non-corporeal Extraterrestrials, etc.), Astral Realms (conscious thoughtforms), and of course, the Physical Realm (Animal, Plant, Mineral and Elemental Kingdoms). A guide to these areas of investigation, and suggested processes for their exploration is provided in my 2015 book, *"Spiritual Journeys."*

SUMMARY

Up to this point, I have provided only a small glimpse into the wide variety of processes and techniques that are are available that would allow you to gain conscious access to your Spiritual Area and then, if you wish, to begin exploring it further. I have discussed only those techniques that I have personally experienced as a client, and have then gone on to become Certified to provide the technique to others. Only in this way, would I have at least a good working knowledge and understanding about their procedures and outcomes, and whether or not they are beneficial and effective for me. With these caveats, the following is a relative comparison of the ease of practice and benefit that each of the techniques discussed has been to me; however, you will need to decide whether or not you wish to pursue any of these, or to find another pathway for your own spiritual journey.

Yes/No Techniques

Pendulum

Pro: Easy to learn how to select and program your pendulum. Fun to use to obtain binary (Yes/Positive/True or No/Negative/False) answers to questions from your 'inner wisdom'.

Con: Validity of Yes or No answers is critically dependent upon your intention and skill in properly programming your pendulum and asking the right questions. Each question must be very simple, specific, and have only one unambiguous answer for which it has been programmed. No shades of gray are allowed in the answer.

Interactive Techniques

ILC Meditation

Pro: An excellent guided visualization for all types of people (e.g., visual, auditory, kinesthetic), as well as for the analytical types who have trouble emptying or clearing the mind. This meditation keeps the conscious mind actively engaged in the rapid vivid imagery and subconscious metaphors that takes them through their physical world into their spiritual awareness and 'up' into their inner wisdom. This meditation technique has proved to be foundational for development of other more advanced and focused programs such as for spiritual healing (Trans-Scalar Healing) and Spiritual Exploration (Spiritual Journeys). After the successful 40-Day Journey, a shortened 19-minute version is available to allow you to spend more time in the room chosen to work in that day (Healing Room, Hall of Records, Learning Room or Meditation Room). The 36-minute "40-Day Journey" meditation and the 19-minute "ILC Meditation" audio tracks, plus a complete manual describing all the symbolic metaphors can be downloaded for free using the link on my website, www.howardbatie.com.

Con: According to Rev. Solomon's instructions, the 36-minute CD for the ILC 40-Day Journey must initially be listened to at least once a day for 40 *consecutive* days. Some people may not be able to make this length of time available in the morning or evening each day, depending on whether they are more alert in the morning or in the evening. A high degree of intention and perseverance is normally needed; however, the results are extremely positive.

Trans-Scalar Healing

Pro: A very powerful and effective program for rapidly accelerating the practitioner's intuitive development and ability to consciously access their Spiritual Area using only focused intention and easy-to-use breathwork techniques. No hypnotic techniques are used. Teaches the practitioner how to become proficient with remote healing techniques where the client is not in your physical presence. Can also be used for local healing sessions where the client is in the practitioner's physical presence. Rapidly develops the ability to consciously communicate and interact with the Healing Angels. It is not necessary to consciously know what the client's healing objectives are; in fact, it is better for the practitioner's own intuitive development if they do not know, and operate "blindly." Prior training in any formal energy healing technique such as Reiki, Healing Touch, Theta Healing, etc. is not required, but may be quite useful. Teaches the student how to develop and use a Scalar Energy field for healing themselves and others. Incorporates a powerful Planetary Healing Process for healing Mother Earth and the Collective Consciousness of Humanity in addition to bringing healing energies to the client.

Can be performed anywhere, at any time (a formal office setting is not required). All materials for learning and teaching this program to others are free and can be downloaded using a link that is provided on my website, howard@howardbatie.com. A complete instruction manual is provided in the book, *"Trans-Scalar Healing: Holistic Healing For Self, Others And Gaia,"* available from Amazon.com (search for "Howard Batie").

Con: A computer that can view the 72-minute narrated PowerPoint Microsoft PowerPoint presentation is required to introduce this self-teaching program and all its processes and procedures in Step 1 of the technique. Step 2 consists of downloading and listening to a free mp3 file from my website. A detailed step-by-step manual for Step 3 is available from Amazon.com (search for "Howard Batie"). It takes practice to learn how to simultaneously operate in 3D and 5D for short periods of time where the practitioner can receive a short visual or audible bit of information in 5D, open their eyes, jot down a note in 3D, close their eyes, and continue in a highly expanded sate of awareness. Although this advanced program is freely made available to everyone, some may find a rather steep initial learning curve as they practice the self-learning procedures; however, persistence and practice have yielded extremely positive results.

Life Between Lives (LBL) Hypnotherapy

Pro: The internationally-acclaimed Life Between Lives (LBL) Hypnotherapy technique was developed and refined by the late Dr. Michael Newton, a conventionally-trained Clinical Psychologist and Certified Hypnotherapist, and is taught only to other Certified Hypnotherapists by the highly experienced training staff at The Newton Institute (TNI) of LBL Hypnotherapy. Trained LBL Hypnotherapist Practitioners are available in over 40 countries (as of 2018) and provide individual client sessions in 20 languages. A comprehensive and thorough introduction to the Spiritual World of the client's own Higher Self is provided in a single session where they will be in deep hypnosis for several hours. All sessions are recorded and the client receives an audio copy of their session. The hypnotic technique itself and the consistent positive results that it achieves are documented in Dr. Newton's books, *"Journeys of the Souls: Case Studies of Life Between Lives,"* and *"Destiny of Souls: New Case Studies of Life Between Lives."* Additional case studies from LBL Practitioners around the world are also available in book format. TNI supports additional research into the experiences of both LBL Practitioners' and clients' own spiritual experiences. TNI also supports a Facebook page where the public can interact with trained LBL Practitioners to have questions answered. The TNI website (www.newtoninstitute.org) provides additional information, as well as a "Locate An LBL Practitioner" link.

Con: Authentic LBL sessions can be provided only by a Hypnotherapist who has been specifically trained and Certified by The Newton Institute. Individual sessions are lengthy, usually about three to four hours. Currently, all LBL clients are provided approximately the same journey through their individual activities in the spiritual realms; however, the results of each journey are always highly individual and personally relevant. Follow-on sessions to delve deeper into the events experienced during your LBL session must currently be separately provided outside the TNI format; however, your LBL Hypnotherapist will probably be the most capable and highly-trained Hypnotherapist you could find to assist you in your continuing spiritual explorations.

Spiritual Journeys

Pro: Spiritual Journeys is a powerful and flexible three-session Program that initially teaches the student how to hypnotize themselves very deeply so that their conscious mind is still aware, but is not doubting what they become aware of, and then teaches them how to consciously access their Spiritual Area. The student can use this ability to relax deeply any time they want, and for a variable length of time that they choose: 10 seconds for practice, 20 minutes for deep meditation, eight hours for a good night's sleep, or for any length at all. This program has a very high success rate for teaching clients to reach their Spiritual Area (99% of my clients). They are taught how to consciously and safely channel (communicate in a two-way dialog or question-answer session) any time they wish. Initially, they are taught how to communicate with their own Higher Self and Spirit Guide, and later with continued practice, with any spiritual being they wish, e.g., Archangels, Angels, Ascended Masters, etc. The student is taught the proper challenging and banishment procedures to ensure their safety and protection against any astral or energetic intruders or deceivers. Private, individual sessions are normally recorded, and a digital copy provided. Additional optional pathways are available for further separate exploration if desired: (1) learning spiritual healing techniques that incorporate Angelic assistance for individuals and for Mother Earth, (2) consciously recalling significant milestones in their own spiritual history (the Personal Akashic Record), and (3) investigating literally any information or event that has ever been recorded in the Universal Akashic Record. Program materials that teach the Spiritual Journeys process are freely made available to Certified Hypnotherapists only; however, a descriptive 19-minute overview of the technique is publicly available on YouTube (search for "Evergreen Healing Arts Center"). A detailed step-by-step manual/book "*Spiritual Journeys: A*

Practical Methodology for Accelerated Spiritual Development and Experiential Exploration" that describes what will be experienced in each of the Spiritual Journeys is available to the public on Amazon.com (search for "Howard Batie").

Con: Anyone can become a Spiritual Journeys client and even learn to reliably channel if they wish; however, in order to provide Spiritual Journeys sessions to others, you must be a Certified Hypnotherapist, since the first thing you will teach your clients is how to hypnotize themselves. Three separated hypnotherapy sessions, about a week apart, are required for the basic foundational ability of being able to consciously communicate with any spiritual being desired. The ability to consciously have an extended conversation with one's own Higher Self and retrieve complex information without assistance is a learned ability that takes persistence and practice.

Chapter 4
Validation Of Channeled Information

This chapter investigates and discusses the methods that have been used to discern whether or not the information received through different human channels is valid; is also discusses the assumptions upon which this discernment is based to "separate the wheat from the chaff." The concept of Accuracy also needs to be discussed because Validity and Accuracy are two different things. In the English language, "Accuracy" is defined by Webster's New Collegiate Dictionary as "Freedom from mistake or error, conformity to truth, exactness," and "Validity" is defined as "Being at once relevant and meaningful... supported or corroborated on a sound or authoritative basis."

So, in order for a statement to be "accurate", it must first be truthful, and for it to be "truthful", it must first be "real, unchanging (constant), and be neither derivative nor dependent". "Real" is defined as, among other uses, "having objective and independent existence." According to these dictionary definitions, absolute accuracy of channeled information cannot be determined by the scientific method, since it does not have an objective existence that can be examined, analyzed, scrutinized, and measured; a purist might discard the information altogether as unscientific and, therefore, merely hearsay and unimportant. However, the report of a fire is also initially merely hearsay, but could also be hugely relevant and important – it certainly should be investigated to determine the validity of the report. This is also the approach needed when exploring channeled information.

Internal Validation

In my two-step approach to validating verbally channeled information, the first step is to examine the internal consistency of the information as it passes through each of the three elements of the channeling process: (1) the Source of the information that is provided telepathically to the Channel's Higher Self, (2) the experience, knowledge and vocabulary of the Channel, and (3) the experience, knowledge and vocabulary of the Director.

Identifying The Source. Let us look at the initial steps in validating channeled information, regardless of the format or modality that is used to provide the information to a client or the public. First, one must be sure of the Source's identification and its spiritual status as a reliable source of information or guidance. As a general rule, Astral Entities from the 4th Dimension of Consciousness (see Appendix B) should be avoided since these levels are full of Tricksters and Deceivers, if not the outright Dark Force Entities of the lower 4th Dimension. The Challenging and Banishment procedures outlined in Chapter 3 should be used to ensure that you are connected to spiritual beings who can provide truthful information.

Higher Selves are excellent sources of information about experiences they have personally had in the spiritual realms, as well as their previous physical incarnations on Earth and potentially other worlds as well. They are all familiar with telepathic modes of information exchange used in the 5th Dimension of Consciousness and higher where feeling and intentions are an integral part of the telepathic exchange, so the information exchanged is automatically based on that Higher Self's Truth, and deception cannot occur.

Ascended Masters are conscious spirit essences who have previously incarnated on a physical world, learned the lessons that physicality can teach, and have remained in the spirit world close to Earth at this time to provide energetic support and guidance to humans to assist the current global collective ascension process of humanity. Ascended Masters, Archangels, Elohim, the Akashic Record, and even Creator Itself are all considered excellent sources of spiritual information on any topic we can think of or even imagine, and these higher sources only await our invitation to participate in a directed verbal channeling session.

Translating The Information. The Second step in the internal validation process is to determine if the Channel has the experience, understanding and vocabulary to accurately translate the telepathic information received from the Source into words that can be spoken or written in the Earth language of the Channel. This is the place where the greatest probability exists that the Source's intentions may become misunderstood or misinterpreted. Much of the way the spiritual realms normally operate, according to them, is beyond the ability of the human brain to understand, and the Source will generally use metaphors and examples to explain some processes. Examples include the way information is simultaneously and instantly processed from several individual beings in a Group Consciousness Entity, or the way energetic 'packets' of information instantaneously contain all the feelings, emotions and nuances of an individual experience. Spiritual sources of information consistently state that they are all very concerned that this translation process from themselves to the Higher Self of the Channel is clear and is understood in a way that allows the Higher Self to connect to the brain's language and vocabulary to accurately express the entire meaning of the original information. As noted before, the Source will often ask, "Is this clearly understood?" or "Am I being clear?"

I am not aware of any absolutely fool-proof way for recognizing whether this translation process is accomplished as intended by the Source. However, the more a Director and Channel work together, each will begin to recognize when the channeled information "feels right" and also whether it seems to be consistent with the Channel's previously provided information, the use of phrases and idioms, and ability to express complex thoughts, feelings and images. So, the experience of working together as a team will be a large factor in this second step of determining the internal validity of the information.

Understanding The Information. The Third step in the internal validation process is that the Director must accurately comprehend the meaning of the message that the Source intended to send. As the Channel is speaking the information, the Channel's Higher Self is translating that spiritual information from the concepts it is given – the visual images it sees, and the feelings it senses – into the vocabulary and words of the Channel; the Director must remain fully conscious to comprehend the intention and meaning of the words the Channel is speaking, and this is the singular strength of the three-participant interactive verbal channeling session. If there is any confusion or misunderstanding on the part of the Director, he or she can immediately ask for clarification or additional explanation using a different example or metaphor.

If there is a significant measure of consistency in the meaning and relevance of the information or message, even if not total congruence on all levels of the details, my belief is that this consistency tends to support the overall validity of the information itself.

External Validation

The final step in the information validation process is to compare the transcript of each channeling session with the transcripts of other sessions that the Channel has conducted. Is the information consistent? Does it support or contradict previous information on the same topic from the same Channel? When channeling the same Source on a different topic, does the use of verbiage and idioms appear the same or different? When channeling different Sources on the same topic, is the use of verbiage and idioms similar? Is the information on the same topic from different Sources supportive or contradictory? And finally, how does the information on a specific topic (e.g., Telepathy and Teleportation) from a specific Source (e.g., Archangel Michael) compare with the information provided through a different Channel to a different Director? If there is a significant measure of consistency in the meaning and relevance of the information or message, even if not total congruence on all levels of the details, my belief is that this consistency tends to support the overall validity of the information itself.

While developing the book, *"The ETs Speak: Who We Are And Why We're Here,"* I had the opportunity to meet and dialogue with representatives of several extraterrestrial civilizations on the same subject: the potential plans being made in the higher dimensions for Disclosure of the presence of 'off-worlders' or beings from other worlds. The measure of consistency from all the representatives interviewed concerning possible Disclosure options was so high that a strong sense of confidence in the information was felt; however, it was also recognized that a final decision had not yet been made. My conversation with one particular representative from the Andromedan Galaxy on the topic of truth and validity of channeled information was also particularly instructive:

Howard: *Welcome, Kyton. Are you a representative of the Galactic Federation?*

Kyton: *Yes. I speak with authority for the Galactic Federation and am the Arbiter of Truth. There is so much information constantly coming from all directions, so much information, actual readings that can be taken at various places by instruments and mathematical equations, there's speech… there's just a constant bombardment of information, and it's very, very important to the Galactic Federation to be sure that everything they put forth and everything they act upon is absolutely correct because there is truth and falsehood, and some of it even is intentionally perpetrated falsehood. We're working toward everyone aiming only for truth, the purity of truth. There are beings in the galaxy that are unable to reach this level of truth, unwilling or they think they know more than they really know. I test this. I'm one of the figures that determines what is truth and what has not evolved to a level of truth.*

You tend to think the galaxies are separate – there's the Milky Way galaxy, the Andromeda galaxy, all the other galaxies, and to an extent, that's true. But there is more overlap than you realize. I'm an Andromedan who also has influence in the Milky Way. I've been asked by Ascended Master St. Germain to come to the Milky Way galaxy to assist, which I gladly did. I came to teach, and to do some arbitration myself. But also, to teach others how to detect truth, how to test for truth, because there are so many levels of deceptions, ways to deceive, so much self-deception. Some of it is very right-hearted in that people want to believe, and they strive so hard toward the truth that

120

they are willing to settle for less than the whole truth. Another of my purposes is to give people the rock-hard heart so that they will accept nothing but the pure truth. Sometimes finding truth is not easy; you have to work and work and go through levels and levels and reams of information in order to find what is actually the truth, and therefore the basis of further action. The Galactic Federation exists to bring truth and a firm basis to the entire universe so they can act with confidence about what they do and make decisions for lesser beings, evolving beings, about how to best bring everything to its highest good and highest growth potential. You can't do this without knowing what is true because truth is the rock we start with. You reach another level; you reach a higher truth or truth that feeds the truth we are working with. Truth is such a nebulous term, I almost hesitate to use it. What is true? Truth is pure, it is hard, and it is one. It has no conflicting parts within it.

This conversation resulted in an even higher level of confidence in the validity of the information transferred from higher dimensional Sources, whether an Extraterrestrial or an Archangel, to the Channel' Higher Selves during all our Spiritual Research Group channeling sessions. Each higher dimensional Source with whom we have communicated has repeatedly expressed concern that their message be clearly and accurately transmitted to and understood by the humans receiving it, and shared as appropriate with others.

The procedures used by our Spiritual Research Group for sharing our channeled information are provided at Appendix C.

Chapter 5
A Multidimensional Experience

Information is not knowledge.
The only source of knowledge is experience,
And you need experience to gain wisdom.
But imagination is more important than knowledge,
For knowledge is limited to all we now know and understand,
while imagination embraces the entire world,
and all there ever will be to know and understand.

~ Albert Einstein

Imagination is 5th Dimensional Thinking.

~ Archangel Michael

In the previous Chapters, I have provided some information about several experiences with my energy healing and Hypnotherapy clients; I have also summarized several modalities by which we can individually and collectively expand our appreciation and awareness of the greater fundamental spiritual nature of which I believe we are all an important part. However, the words you have read absolutely pale in comparison to the actual experiences that my clients, students and I have felt and known along our individual Journeys; such is the limitation of language. Nevertheless, in this chapter, I will attempt to describe an important experience of my own that is now, to me, unquestionably very real **know**ledge of who I am and why I am here on Earth at this time.

I am fortunate in that I have learned to pay attention to the occasional "nudge" I get from my own Higher Self where doing something that I'm thinking of results in a "good feeling" or a "Yes" and I've also learned to recognize when that feeling in the pit of my stomach says, "Watch out!" or "No". Several times during my lifetime I was aware that I was being guided or led by some higher power to a certain objective, and that if I allowed myself to listen to the guidance that was being provided, the results would be a beneficial in some way for me. It always turned out to be exactly that, so I learned to pay attention to those nudges.

On a Thursday at the end of April 2015, my wife Anita, who is a very accomplished artist in many media, was attending a 5-day workshop about 160 miles away for about 400 artists from all over the world. In the middle of this time, I recall going down our steep 150-foot long driveway to get the mail, and when I began to go back up the driveway, I suddenly felt quite dizzy and out of breath for a moment, and 'heard' someone close by shout very clearly, "Watch Out!" A quick look around showed I was completely alone with no one within 200 yards, so I just thanked "The Voice" again and stood for a moment to catch my breath.

All sorts of thoughts began to race through my mind - at the tender young age of 75, was I having a heart attack? No, I don't think so, but why don't my legs move very well? I almost feel a bit nauseous, so I'd better not move too fast. In fact, it IS a bit hard to catch my breath, so I'd better just not move at all right now! Don't panic, just remain calm... The Calming Tool! I thought of the Calming Tool, one of the self-hypnosis techniques in my toolbox that I had developed to help my clients instantly calm themselves in moments of anxiety and worry. I'll do the Calming Tool! As I touched my right thumb and middle finger together to form a circle, I thought of the magic word I had taught my students when they were in deep hypnosis. Instantly, I FELT a wave of relaxing calmness move quickly down through me from the top of my head to the tip of my toes, and I immediately let go of the anxiety and stress that was beginning to build up and cause my heart to race. I feel it now slowing down quite a bit.

But I'm not "out of the woods" yet – I still have a long climb back uphill to our home, so I begin very slowly, one step at a time and then rest, repeat one more step up and rest; eventually I climb back up the driveway, get into the house and quite calmly call my doctor's office. As usual, the doctor is busy, but the lady I was talking to (a Nurse? Probably not.) very politely says that I should go to the specific nearby medical clinic she mentioned and at least have an electro-cardiogram (EKG) taken. I tell her I will do that, hang up, and immediately start saying all the MBOs (Most Benevolent Outcomes) I could think of to ask my Angels get me through this experience OK. More Calming Tool. Breathe deeply and slowly!

No one else is at home with me, but it's only a short 6-mile drive to the nearest medical clinic. More MBOs for a safe drive. I slowly and calmly walk in to the front desk and tell them I'd like to have an EKG taken since I'm experiencing shortness of breath and bit of dizziness. The medical clinic tells me they don't have a EKG machine, and that I'd should go to a different neighborhood medical clinic adjacent to an assisted living complex – they are sure to have an EKG machine there. More MBOs and Calming Tool. Another short 5-mile drive and the recommended medical clinic says Yes, they have an EKG machine, but all they can do is get a readout of how my heart is doing. They couldn't provide any further medical care if it is needed – so I need to go to the Emergency Room at the local hospital that has both the EKG facilities and the staff to provide any indicated medical care.

Then it hit me like a ton of bricks! Why didn't I think of doing that in the first place? More Calming Tool! I realize that I am probably in some state of shock with the possibility of a mortal crisis, and my analytical brain isn't really functioning very well. More MBOs... Angels, please get me to the hospital without any more drama! Another 8-mile drive to the hospital, and I calmly walk up to the receptionist and ask if I could get an EKG because I'm beginning to show the signs of CHF, (Congestive Heart Failure). Those must be magic code words. She probably hit a little red button somewhere, because a nurse immediately bursts out of the double doors of the triage room, flies out of with a wheelchair, plunks me down in it, and wheels me into the EKG room where at least a dozen little probes are attached to my chest in a flurry of activity. A Physician comes in, looks at the EKG strip and orders me to be immediately admitted. Evidently it was worse than I thought, and I thank the Angels again for getting me here. More Calming Tool and more MBOs.

Well, here I am in my hospital room, very relaxed with the light sedative I've been given, so I use my cell phone and call the retreat center where my wife, Anita, is attending her workshop. They say they will try to locate her and hang up. A little while later Anita calls me and says she'll immediately leave and be there at the hospital in about 3 hours or so. Meanwhile, the doctors are recommending that a probe be sent up from my leg artery to my heart to inspect things, and they think that a stent would likely solve any problems they find. But instead, they find three cardiac arteries that are nearly completely blocked, so a stent was out, and I would have to be transferred to the nearest hospital that does heart surgery, about 30 miles away, for what they call a 'cabbage' – CABG, med-speak for Coronary Artery Bypass Graft. Ambulance transport was arranged for the next day, Friday, May 1. More sedatives, more MBOs and more Calming Tool!

At the new hospital, I am told that the heart surgeons have a full schedule, and the earliest they could get to me would be Monday, so I spend the weekend lightly sedated with happy drugs and calmed with the Calming Tool. Finally! Monday comes and the nurse arrives to prep me with, among other things, a bit more sedation. I kissed Anita and, as they were wheeling me into the operating room, I remember asking the nurse what time it was; she said, "It 10:30am, May the Fourth... be with you!" I relaxed totally with a smile and said, "Thank you for that!" That is the last thing I remember before the operation, but it's certainly only the beginning of the most powerful experience I have ever had.

Without any sense or feeling that time had passed, I am now looking down through an irregular 'hole' in the ceiling where I see several people around my physical body lying there on the operating table. There is a lot of movement as people respond to the surgeon's directions to hand him an instrument, open the chest a bit further, stop that bit of bleeding there, check with the Anesthesiologist, etc., and I marvel at how swiftly and professionally everyone is working together, just as if they were a single being getting everything done just right. Then I hear the surgeon say, "I think we need another graft around this one that's about 85% blocked. Might as well do it right now – that makes it a four-way bypass."

Then I feel something happening in the back of my head ... as I look down at my body, I somehow just know that a tiny part of my brain stops working. I look up and see another man looking at me with infinite love and concern. He is about four or five feet in front of me, dressed completely in white – white coat, white pants, white shirt, white tie, even white hair, but his skin is lightly tanned and his eyes are the bluest I've ever seen. I look down at his shoes to see if they were also white, but he doesn't have any feet or shoes at all; for that matter, I don't either! He looks to be about 45 or so, and as I look at myself (how did I do that?), I seem to be about 35 or so, and both of us appear very healthy, trim and fit. All of a sudden, I am observing this 'Greeter' in white from about four feet behind him and off to his left side, and I look at myself standing about eight feet away facing Mr. Greeter, so I can see myself very clearly; then, from behind Mr. Greeter, I hear him say to the me in front of him, "You now have a choice. You can come Home with me, or you can return to your body and to your life. What do you choose to do?"

Well, I think that it is very curious that I am behind Mr. Greeter, while I see the other me over there observing my body below, but then I instantly thought, "I'll figure that out later. I have to make a choice NOW!" If there was time, it stopped completely. As I look down below at my body again, I know that it is damaged somehow and would never work again as well as it had before, and if I choose to return to my body, I would be somehow impaired physically. At the same time, I feel an extremely strong, loving, magnetic force pulling me backward and upward to go 'Home' with Mr. Greeter. In the same instant, as I observed this conversation from behind Mr. Greeter who was facing the other me who was thinking about what to choose, I 'hear' myself silently think, "Hmmm, it will be very interesting to see what he (the other me) decides to do!" Then, I looked at myself over there standing in front of the Greeter, looked down again at my body on the table, saw my wife Anita in my mind, and heard that other me say, "No, there are some things I would still like to do in this lifetime, so I choose to return to my body and my life." At that instant, I had no idea what those things were that I still had to do, but I was quite positive that I just wanted the opportunity to continue living to do them.

My next awareness was groggily trying to open my eyes. Anita was there and I heard her say from far away, "He's awake now!" As I slowly adjusted to being in my body again, I began trying out my legs and arms to make sure that everything worked again: Left hand - Yes! Left arm - Check! Left leg - Yes, toes wiggle, too! Right hand, not so much. Right arm, nothing. Right leg, oops - not working at all. I think this is very interesting and curious, and I hear me say, "Hey, Honey – look at this, I'm trying to move my right arm and leg and they're not working yet!" Then I hear Anita shouting for the nurse and telling her that she thinks I've had a stroke! I think to myself, "Uh-oh! Well, this is what I chose to return to!"

In the next couple of days, I had several Computerized Tomography (CT) and Magnetic Resonance Imaging (MRI) scans to determine the extent of the damage caused by the stroke; the Neurologist assigned to my case said that I had experienced three blockages in the blood vessels in the back part of my brain, the region that was responsible for motor movement of my limbs, and that sometimes stroke patients also experienced a tightening of the throat muscles and slurring of speech. Two weeks of in-patient physical therapy was followed by another four weeks of out-patient physical therapy, and eventually, I could haltingly walk around again with only a slight limp, but only for a short time and distance. But I also soon found that I could not speak continuously for more than about 10 minutes before my throat felt like it was tightening up and closing shut. So, at least I know the physical limitations that I will be working with after I am completely discharged. And I was also still wondering who, or what part of me, was that observer who was aware of the conversation between Mr. Greeter and the other me?

And what else did I learn from this experience? I've heard it said that there are no coincidences, and that everything happens for a reason. I've also previously heard in my spiritual regression training that before we are born, the spiritual part of each one of us chooses the family into which we will be born, the parents who will raise us, the lessons we are to learn during our lifetime, and also how and when we will exit our lifetime and 'graduate' from this earthly University of Life. But it was my very vivid Out-Of-Body-*Experience* (OOBE) and Near-Death Experience (NDE) described above that taught me several things about Life and about Death.

First, I learned, in a way that I now firmly KNOW, that my future death is nothing to fear, and will not be the end of my consciousness' existence; Second, my 'graduation' will be like easily moving from a small, dimly lit room into a vibrant, large, life-filled room of love, peace and joy like I've done many times before; Third, I confirmed the existence of a spiritual 'Greeter' being who escorts Home those souls whose body has died and helps them to adjust to the greater reality of their spiritual and energetic being; Fourth, I confirmed the existence of pre-chosen 'Exit Points' where my Higher Self or soul would have the choice of returning Home or extending my physical lifetime contract to some future Exit Point; and Fifth, upon reviewing my OOBE, I believe my 5th Dimensional Higher Self was looking at and sensing my 3rd Dimensional body on the operating table, and then an even higher aspect of my consciousness (10th or 15th Dimensional?) was also wondering whether my 5th Dimensional Self would choose to go Home or to return to the body. I now understand what being 'Multi-Dimensional' really means – consciously being aware that I simultaneously exist in more than just one dimension of consciousness at the same time!

More recently, I wanted to verify that the information I had believed about my Greeter and the Exit Points was in fact valid; therefore, I participated in an SRG session where I was the

Director and my own Higher Self was the Source. My conscious conversation with Artoomid, the name that my own Higher Self has chosen to use, was through one of my trained Channels, and the purpose was to either confirm or refute my prior conclusions regarding my OOBE and NDE experiences. Our conversation was:

Howard: Artoomid, I'm reviewing the process that I went through, and the images that I received, during my Heart Bypass Operation, and I still have some questions that have not been answered by the medical community. First, during my Heart Operation, did my heart stop?

Artoomid: *For a little while, yes. It stopped on its own, but the physician felt he was in control, and was not concerned. He knew he could "bring it back". You may think that your body died, but it was not beyond repair. There is a time or a space in which the body physically functions, even though the heart has quit, and as long as the body is cared for, and assisted to receive oxygen, it can maintain what you consider "life" for a little while without the heart. But the heart needs to circulate the blood very soon. Your surgeon was aware that it had stopped, and he was able to quickly get it "re-beating". I see he used a pressure, not exactly a jolt, but a strong physical "squeezing" to trigger the heart to move again.*

Howard: Good. During that time when my heart stopped, I became aware of what I call an "Out of body experience". After I woke up, I remembered looking down through the ceiling, and watching my physical body on the table.

Artoomid: *Yes. Michael and I both were letting you know that you would soon reach a point where you*

*would have a choice, and that your brain had suffered,
but it was not beyond repair. And you would be given
a choice to come back to a body that would take a lot
of work and lot of dedication to bring back, and it was
your Soul's choice. You think of it as "out of body", but
it is a place that you can go to at any point, once you
gain that control. You were there because you were
at a juncture, so to speak, a point of choice.*

Howard: What I became aware of was a man who looked
to be physical, looked to be dressed in white, white pants,
white shirt. Was I imagining this person, or was there a
spiritual "greeter" of some sort there? Who was this being
that appeared in my mind?

Artoomid: *He was there to accompany you if you
chose to leave your body behind. He is one whom
you know on the other side. He is one who has
volunteered to assist you in the past when you have
left the physical body, and he will return when you do
decide to move on. He is what you may think of as a
"Tour Guide" or a "Wayshower" as you move on. He
is there waiting on the other side and observing. He is
performing this assistance to many, and is considered
as assistance for moving forward and back. He does
this for not just one Soul, and this is his specialty. As
you make the transition, he is there to hold your hand
or guide you forward without fear. He is dressed in
white as a comfort to you, as there is a soul memory
for you that is positive for this type of appearance, and
it is a calming sight for your Soul.*

Howard: Alright. Now during this Out Of Body
Experience, he asked me a question: "What do you choose
to do, return to the body, or come home with me?" Is this

132

the choice that's given to everyone who is in the process of transitioning?

Artoomid: *Only to those whose physical body can be returned to. There are those to whom the body has been essentially lost. It has been damaged or has aged to the point that it cannot really be repaired. They do not have a choice; they must move on. But if your body can sustain you longer, and you wish to return to do further work, you may return, and that is the choice you were given.*

Howard: During this experience with the Greeter, I was also aware that I was standing behind the greeter, and off to his left, behind him. I was observing the other "me" who was looking down at my body. What part of my consciousness was standing behind the Greeter, observing the other me?

Artoomid: *You have been introduced to exactly what is meant by "multi-dimensionality", or the ability to observe from many different perspectives. The "you" that was watching the body closely, was the part of the Soul Essence that is deeply imbedded into the physical body and is used to maintain and control and be within that body, and that part is the part of the consciousness that simply observes, that is not the physical, and that is the part that was with the being you call the Greeter. So, they were all parts of you, but from different perspectives of your Soul. You think of me, Artoomid, as your Higher Self, so to speak. I represent that bridge between embodiment in the physical, and a Soul in the etheric and the higher world of non-physicality, and the Higher Self moves back and forth between. So, the Higher Self, yes, is* *observing and was that entity, but was also still highly attached to the physical, as well as highly attached to the Superconscious part of you that is non-physical, your Soul. The Higher Self is essentially the link of the entire essence to the particular purpose at that time. The Higher Self is that part of you which directs and gives Soul Energy to the physicality, which observes and interprets and assists with your movement forward and the decisions that you make. The Higher Self is there to assist with your Guides and give nudges, to interpret the happenings in physicality that you use to grow forward. So, the Higher Self is essentially your internal guidance system, that part of you which, when used, can really help you to decide what works best for you. And it, therefore, can access the physical part of you as well as the Higher parts of you to help you.*

Howard: So that was you, then?

Artoomid: *Yes. Michael and I together because, as your Guide, Michael is always there and available, but when you were in such crisis, he was very close to you, and I was with him. You have heard from other channels that once you are in the higher dimensions, you don't have a name, but are recognized by your vibration or your "Light". That is essentially that highest consciousness part of you, and that is what you are describing, your consciousness, or your Soul, your basic "who you are". You, as a Soul, are extended into Artoomid, which is represented in physicality as Howard.*

Howard: My linear brain is trying to equate my physical body as third dimensional, Artoomid is my fifth dimensional Higher Self, and this other part of my consciousness is higher -- seventh, eighth, or whatever. Does that make sense?

Artoomid: *Yes. That is exactly how it is. You mentioned earlier the differences in dimensions, and it is easier to understand from that perspective of that part of your consciousness or Soul, that it is able to represent itself in more than one dimension of consciousness, and it can simultaneously access more than one dimension. And as it learns and grows and gains more understanding of the dimensions themselves, it can vibrate at a faster and faster or higher and higher level, and therefore can access more and more information, which is considered from your perspective, to be higher dimensions. So, it isn't step by step by step, but more of an expansion outward in waves. I am you, and I am that part of you that is your best friend, that is closest to knowing who and what you really are, and how you really serve. You are one of those who is aware and has memories of having been momentarily separated from your physical body, and able to return to it, and it is good to share with others, so that it calms the fears of those who are unsure about what happens when one transitions. It helps for others to understand that it is not the end, but is merely a change, or in truth, a movement forward.*

Howard: So, I believe that this was, in fact, a "Near-Death Experience." Is that correct?

Artoomid: *Yes. It was more than just an Out Of Body Experience. You had the choice, at that point, to transition. So that is as near death that you get* *without transitioning!*

Howard: I've heard this point of transitioning described by some as being at an "Exit Point". Are these Exit Points chosen by my Higher Self, or by my Soul, before I incarnate?

Artoomid: *In general, yes. There is a belief that our whole life is predetermined by our Soul. But rather, the circumstances of that life are chosen because they will provide the best opportunities for those lessons. There are times when part of that lesson is perhaps a death at a young age, and that was foreseen by the Soul as part of the lesson. But there are also choices that can be made as a life nears an ending or time when the body begins to fail, where you may continue or choose to transition, based on your own comfort level with what you have learned here. So, you may be given a choice, or you may not. That does not happen for all Souls. There are Souls that are unaware, and they often experience a death that they see as unplanned, but that the Soul had (planned) before it happened. But it is not always that your Soul knew that on a certain date you would have a heart attack and that you would die or not die; but the Soul may know that you have choices as you reach those ages, and that those choices would still be left open until that time occurred. Your Soul did not necessarily know that you would choose to continue, but your Soul may have been well aware that you would be given that choice at that time.*

Howard: Yes. I recall very vividly thinking that it will be very curious to see what "he" chooses.

Artoomid: *Yes. And that "he" is a perspective from your core Soul, so to speak. You are given the opportunities, and you have free will to make the choice, and the Soul, once you make that choice, will guide you forward from there.*

Howard: Alright. And I made the choice, obviously, to return because I felt there was something I still needed to do.

Artoomid: *Yes. And you ARE doing it, Howard. Do not doubt that.*

Howard: Good. Thank you, Artoomid. There is another aspect of this experience that I'd like to explore. (Higher Self of Channel), I'd like you to call Michael to come forward. (Pause)

Higher Self of Channel: He is here, and it is him.

Howard: Welcome, Michael! Thank you for coming. I was surprised, pleased but surprised, that you also were there observing my near-death experience, and I'm curious about what role did you have to play, that Artoomid was not able to, or capable of performing?

Michael: *It was more that Artoomid and I were there to observe you as you moved through this event in your life and made your choice; and to be available to you, depending upon the choice that you made. We were both there, offering our strength through Soul Energy, and our comfort for you, to help you to rise above and to observe, and to remain calm as you did so. But we were not influencing your choice, other than to make you aware that the choice was there for you. We were not hastening the event, nor were we*

137

slowing it down. We were allowing it to occur as it needed to occur for you, and then we were there in support, to be available depending upon whatever choice you made. So, if you chose to go with the person that you call the "Greeter", we would have been there, as well, to help you move along your path forward. As you chose to stay, we were delighted to assist you to come back into yourself, and to have the strength to be willing to make the changes, or to put in the energy to allow that body to be functional enough that you could continue on your path in third dimension. So, we were not making things happen, but we were there observing and being an internal strength for you. I am always there with you, Howard. I am always observing you. I come directly to communicate with you only when you ask for it, but I am always there observing.

Howard: Alright. Thank You!

Since I am here writing this, and you are here reading my words, it is quite apparent that, during my OOBE/NDE, I exercised my free will choice and elected to 'extend my contract,' and returned to my lifetime for some reason. I have since reflected on what that reason could be, and since everything in my current lifetime has really been about the central theme of Communication in one form or another, I have concluded that my Life Purpose for returning is to inform others, through this book and others I have published since my OOBE/NDE, of the many great benefits and methods of establishing conscious communication in a conversational dialog with 'the other side.' This 'other side' is from where we incarnate and to which we return when it is time to take off our physical 'suit'. And as more and more people begin to recognize that, while incarnated, they are also an integral part of the Collective Consciousness of Humanity, hopefully our inter-personal communications will begin to emphasize and support our common abilities and strengths, instead of our perceived differences and assumed limitations. That will be the beginning of Wisdom, both as an evolving individual spiritual consciousness and as the collective physical civilization we called Humankind.

Epilogue

Looking down on Early Earth from Its higher perspective, Creator begins to feel a growing optimism as the universal life force energy anchors itself firmly on a little rock in a far-flung corner of an unremarkable galaxy. Slowly and inexorably, the muck and soup of amino acids and elements of primordial life continue to grow and evolve into oceanic colonies of myriads of different lifeforms, each searching for more food to sustain itself, while unconsciously imprinting the energetic directive of "survival of the fittest" into every cell of their being, usually at the expense of other lifeforms.

A cosmic eyeblink later, and more advanced lifeforms are emerging from their oceanic cradle, finding that the land has already been prepared to sustain them with an abundance of plant life everywhere. And in another instant, thousands of different animal lifeforms have established themselves, with some of them even harboring a nascent intelligence and the ability to use tools to help them find food, as they band together in larger groupings to defend themselves against animals who would prey on them.

Another eyeblink, and these creative children are now using their ingenuity and creativity to build all manner of devices and machines that can even transport them around their beautiful world; however, it is also evident that their technological prowess has surpassed their desire to use their own creations responsibly. Having uncovered the secrets of the atoms, humans have fashioned, and have even chosen to USE, these atomic devices that rip apart the very fabric of third-dimensional space-time, killing thousands of their own kind.

There is much concern that it is now increasingly probable that they could bring the entire human civilization on Earth, their collective consciousness, and even their small, beautiful planet, to the brink of annihilation; yet they continue to create transportation devices that will even take them to other planets. What will they choose to bring with them as they venture across space to distant worlds? Will it be aggressive conquest in their continual lust for more resources, riches and power over others, or will it be wise and compassionate guidance and counsel as they will inevitably meet and interact with other emerging and more advanced civilizations? How can these fledgling spacefarers best learn who and what they really are before they export their havoc throughout their Galaxy and beyond?

After much consideration, the decision is made to block the passage of any further lower-dimensional energies of any kind from moving to Earth or from Earth. In addition, higher-dimensional lines of communication are strongly encouraged to allow the establishment of communication between the awakening human sleepers and their Higher Selves and Spiritual Mentors in a process they call "channeling." In this way, it is hoped that knowledge, wisdom and compassion can begin to balance raw strength, greed and conquest, and will give these brave adventurers the opportunity to become Galactic Emissaries and representatives for peaceful cooperation among all whom they meet as they evolve into an Explorer Race and reach for the stars.

Our Spiritual Discussion Group

During the development of my 2015 book *"Spiritual Journeys: A Practical Methodology for Accelerated Spiritual Development and Experiential Exploration,"* I had trained several dozen clients to access an expanded state of conscious awareness, and to then move their expanded consciousness into their Spiritual Area. They were then coached through a wide variety of their own personal spiritual experiences; this allowed them to access and channel information that related not only to them personally, but also provided significant detailed information about the spiritual realms of awareness, about the spiritual inhabitants of these realms, and about their interactions with each other and with human beings.

It was these clients who urged me to form an informal discussion group of other Spiritual Journeys students so that we could collectively share, discuss and validate in a wider group what they had separately experienced in their individual self-hypnotic sessions. Our "Spiritual Discussion Group" was initially formed in 2013 and gradually expanded to include about thirty like-minded students and clients who have regularly met to share their spiritual experiences. As with most groups, several new members have come to see what our Group is all about, and several have left because of changing interests, moving, new job. etc. We now have a core of about a dozen regular attendees, some of whom have been with us for several years. To each prospective new member, the following information is provided:

Welcome To Our Spiritual Discussion Group!

Purpose. The purpose of our Spiritual Discussion Group (SDG) is to provide a private, supportive forum for like-minded individuals to share and discuss their spiritual experiences as they progress through the several sessions of the Spiritual Journeys Program during this period of Planetary Ascension. If you're looking for a safe, friendly and non-judgmental meeting where you can safely share your personal insights and feelings, you are invited to join us to see for yourself if we can provide the type of atmosphere and information that can support you on your own journey.

The Spiritual Journeys Program has been developed by Howard Batie to significantly accelerate your spiritual development, and then to begin consciously exploring the spiritual realms we all came from and to which we will return when we no longer need our physical 'suits'. With this program, the conscious awareness of your true spiritual nature can be significantly accelerated through the technique of self-hypnosis to allow you to consciously contact and communicate with your own Higher Self and Spirit Guide(s) for practical information to assist you in meeting your daily challenges and opportunities. Once your awareness is able to consciously enter the spiritual realms at will, you can then, under guidance and direction, begin to safely explore and experience any or all of the three areas of interest available: 1 - advanced Angelic and Spiritual Self-Healing sessions that you can also provide to others with Angelic assistance, 2 - conscious recall of your own soul memories in the Personal Spiritual Growth path, and 3 - investigation of nearly anything in this and other universes as you explore the Akashic Record of all events, actions, deeds, objects, and thoughts of all beings in Creation. Further information about the Spiritual

Journeys Program can be found on my website, www.howardbatie.com, in a YouTube overview video (go to YouTube.com, and in their search box, enter "Howard Batie"), and in my August 2015 book "Spiritual Journeys" available on Amazon.com.

Meetings. Our Spiritual Discussion Group currently meets on the second Sunday of each month from 2-4 pm Pacific Time (Seattle or Los Angeles) in a Zoom video teleconference (similar to Skype) in the English language. This allows wide participation by not only local students and clients, but also those who are anywhere in the world. Additionally, audio-only telephone support is provided for those who do not have a video streaming capability. Zoom supports Apple, PC and Linux computers, tablets and both Apple and Android cell phones.

Although initially formed in 2013 to support my Spiritual Journeys clients and students, we welcome anyone interested in sharing their experiences as they continue to grow and evolve as spiritual beings. Our activities and information are not related to or supportive of any religious teachings, but are instead focused on each person's individual *spiritual* growth and development. We emphasize active discussion and exchange of information from a wide variety of sources and topics instead of just one person providing a lecture. Our Group consists of about 25 Members, with about 10 -12 Members who regularly attend each monthly meeting, along with several additional invited Guests. There is no charge or obligation to attend our monthly meetings. Additional interested guests may also be invited to join us simply by expressing interest to howard@howardbatie.com and requesting teleconference access. You are always free to move on to a different sharing group if we do not meet your expectations and needs.

Activities. At each meeting, those attending are invited to share, if they so choose, their personal experiences and insights they have observed in themselves and others during the past month or so. This can be a very important sharing to validate and support the experiences of others as well. We also review interesting and relevant information and messages channeled from and through sources we trust – for example, current messages from the Archangels (e.g., Metatron, Michael, Gabriel, etc.), Ascended Masters (e.g., Jesus / Sananda, Hilarion, Kwan Yin, St. Germain, etc.), and specific Spirit Guides and Higher Selves of individuals who have a long-standing and proven record of providing valid information. Additional articles of current interest (such as the NASA and ESA investigation of the possibilities of life on other planets, the development and use of advanced technologies to help clean up our planet, and conversations with members of the Galactic Federation) are also reviewed and discussed as appropriate.

DropBox. To help facilitate sharing information within our Spiritual Discussion Group, I have created a DropBox account with a folder dedicated to our Spiritual Discussion Group. As we come across interesting internet and magazine articles, messages and channeled information, a copy is placed in the current monthly subfolder, and these are reviewed and discussed at our next Spiritual Discussion Group meeting. If you are a regular Member of our Group, you will be given access to this folder, as well as to the complete archive of previous months' folders as well. We also maintain a group email listing of members; this allows all Group members to exchange interesting information that occurs between monthly meetings that might be worthy of more immediate attention.

Spiritual Research Group (SRG). As the individual members of our Spiritual Discussion Group progressed through the many options available within the Spiritual Journeys Program, several developed the ability to clearly channel information from spiritually evolved sources and from the Universal Akashic Record on nearly any subject or topic at all. These individuals were then invited to participate in the activities of our Spiritual Research Group. Each SRG Member is invited to separately meet in an individual channeling session to further explore the vast spectrum of information that is now available to each one of us, and if the channel permits, the new information and insights can be shared as appropriate with the other members of our Spiritual Research Group and with the regular Members of our monthly Spiritual Discussion Group. We have also developed appropriate protocols and procedures for anonymously sharing selected channeled transcripts with additional Spiritual Discussion Groups as they are formed in other locations around the world.

SRG Information Archive. As each new channeling session is conducted and the session information is transcribed, the entire transcript is entered into our SRG Archive, and the specific topics of investigation covered during each channeling (usually from one to four topics) are added to a Consolidated Spiritual Research Index. This Index of topics is then made available to all regular Members of our SDG, as well as to other Leaders of SDGs which have been established in other communities around the world. Practical procedures have been adopted to facilitate sharing of channeled information both within our own SDG and among all active SDGs, while also honoring the individual channel's desires for anonymity.

The Sources we have channeled include, but are not limited to, Archangels (Metatron, Michael, Gabriel, Raphael, etc.), Ascended Masters (St. Germain, Sananda/Jesus, etc.), Galactic Federation representatives (Ashtar, UFO Commanders, etc.), Spirit Guides, Guardian Angels and Higher Selves of our channels, etc. Specific protocols are always used to ensure that the Channel connects only with these higher dimensional beings, and not with other Astral Realm entities whose motivations and truthfulness are more suspect.

If the above activities and objectives resonate with you and your interests, please consider attending our next Spiritual Discussion

Group Zoom teleconference which is currently meeting from 2-4 pm Pacific Time on the second Sunday of each month, subject to change as necessary. We are always open to meeting and sharing with others who are also learning and growing spiritually!

Blessings,

Howard Batie
Director, Evergreen Healing Arts Center
Chehalis, WA 98532 USA
howard@howardbatie.com https://www.howardbatie.com

There is nothing in the caterpillar that tells you it is going to be a butterfly.

Dimensions of Consciousness

The spiritual realms are host to an infinite number and variety of souls or spiritual beings. Some souls choose to incarnate into a physical body to express their creativity and individuality as human beings on Earth as well as on other worlds, and other souls do not need to associate with a physical body and remain in the spiritual realms as pure consciousness. To additionally complicate matters, several spiritual sources have stated that there are as many as twelve levels of understanding in both the physical world and in the spiritual world. However, it is usually rather difficult for our human physical brain to comprehend and understand a conscious existence in such 'higher' spiritual realms of existence without some form of 'mental roadmap'. Nevertheless, it is important to understand the differences in the amount and type of information that is available from these levels when learning to communicate with residents of each level, whether that communication is verbal or intuitive or telepathic.

Physical Realm Of Form
On February 27, 2016 Archangel Michael provided, through Ronna Herman Vezane, a channeled description of the structure of the first five levels of evolving consciousness (those that most humans are able to comprehend at this time) in a discourse entitled "The Five Kingdoms/Dimensions For This Round Of Earthly Ascension". Each of the Third, Fourth, and Fifth levels or "Dimensions" of consciousness also has seven sub-levels of consciousness, as Archangel Michael has described below. The italicized information is additional insight provided by our Spiritual Research Group during the investigation of the Mineral, Plant and Animal Kingdoms.

First Dimension: The Mineral Kingdom. This is the world of the elements, the fundamental building blocks of the material world from the sub-atomic elements to the soil, rocks, air and water that make up the body of the Earth. The consciousness of the Mineral Kingdom is characterized by simply Being without movement.

The Mineral Kingdom is a layering of the earliest life form, not knowable by the human at this point. Minerals do not need sustenance, but provide that for the beginning of conscious life forms, the plants. They are static, they are knowing without knowing without knowing. Their life awareness is deep, old, and very ancient. They are an ancient entity unto themselves that was created by the Elohim, but they are not intended to communicate with more advanced life forms, other than in their chemical and energetic properties.

Second Dimension: The Plant and Animal Kingdoms. The Plant Kingdom is found on the lower sub-levels of the Second Dimension and is characterized by Growth and Reproduction, but little, if any, physical movement by their structures except for waving in the wind and responding to the position of the sun. As mentioned above, the plants, flowers and trees (the Flora of the Earth) are sustained by the Mineral Kingdom and water from the rivers and rains.

The Plant Kingdom was created to support and bring forth life on Earth and to support more complicated life forms such as animals of all kinds. It gives nurturance of itself as no other life form does for the planet. Its sole purpose is to sustain other life forms, to give back to the air, to provide food and nurturance, and to hold the life energy. It holds life force energy that can be transmitted to other life forms by what it creates, how it interacts, how it feeds, by its making of oxygen. It was given to Earth as a primary form of sustenance, and introduced life and life essence.

There is consciousness in plant life forms, but of a different type. It is aware without being aware. Its purpose is sustenance and support. To be fully conscious would be painful and difficult. It does its job with pure love and joy, as children of Gaia, and so its self-consciousness has been limited to protect it, to keep it from the duality on Earth and the pain, both physical and emotional, of providing sustenance. It is a sacrificial life form of sorts. It asks nothing in return, only to grow and provide, which is its purpose.

As the planet began to develop and Gaia began to develop and grow, and it was determined that there would soon be animal life on this planet, and the Plant Kingdom agreed to provide a variety of life forms to meet the needs of the growing non-plant life and the energetic needs of Gaia in the early days. And so, it began its own diversification project. It grew as needed and continued to meet the needs of the ever-changing, ever-evolving life forms of Gaia and Planet Earth.

Some of the life forms in the Plant Kingdom, such as large trees, serve as sustenance for the growing animal life forms, for they provide shelter and homes, and they carry within them a type of advanced consciousness, and their roots run deep to help connect with Gaia. At one time, trees could awaken if it was necessary to help project energy, to protect, or

151

to assist in the growth of Gaia. Today, they still function in that way; however, they do not awaken.

The flower is a go-between from the Plant Kingdom to the Animal Kingdom. It allows certain species' sustenance and nurturing, and it also provides energy of a high level, something you would call beauty, as raising consciousness levels, and they have become symbolic of that. So, they do provide sustenance for some beings, but in their beauty, they also create such a wonderful energy of love. It is a constant smile of joy, of fragrance.

In the mid and upper levels of the Second Dimension of Consciousness is the Animal Kingdom, which is characterized by Growth, Reproduction and Physical Movement of the animal form. As the Animal Kingdom began to evolve, basic feelings and emotions began to be displayed and experienced as primal fear, anger and instinctual love or compatibility with a strong desire for companionship within their own species. The Animal Kingdom is strongly influenced by inborn instinct, and the animals' consciousness come from and return to a collective consciousness "Group Soul" between each physical lifetime.

Initially, there was a very rudimentary form of life, more like a slime-mold, that evolved from the muck of chemical elements and amino acids; when that was observed, the Angelic Kingdom, the Elohim, Creator, all levels were amazed, and actually excited. It was not expected that these 'pure chemicals' would be able to form life. Instead of waiting for this muck and slime to continue to evolve, it was decided in the councils of Heaven that a more advanced form of consciousness would be given to Gaia, Terra at the

152

time. The reeds and grasses came first, so that animals would have sustenance when they were seeded. There were many worlds that wanted to participate in this Experiment, and they all contributed some of their species of lower life forms that could be adapted to survive on Earth, within the consciousness of Terra. It was decided to experiment with a range of species from many worlds; some were conscious of themselves, and some were just a part of a group consciousness of similar animals.

Third Dimension: Sub-levels 1-3. The lower sublevels of the Third Dimension of Consciousness are composed of certain animals which have developed a limited sentient intelligence, such as the Primates (Apes and Monkeys), Elephants, Horses, Dogs and Cats.

Third Dimension: Sublevels 4-7. The mid and upper sub-levels of the Third Dimension of Consciousness are the lowest level of humankind's experiential existence. As pre-hominids continued to evolve, they exhibited a gradual, limited consciousness of self, as in "I am separate and different from you." Slowly, they emerged from a herd-state consciousness where there were seldom any unique or individualized thoughts, and a more individualized part of their self-awareness became more influential as their ego consciousness developed more fully. Most knowledge came forth from the group instinctual nature and basic concepts handed down from elders within their communities.

Along with the development of sentient self-awareness and a strong egoic component within their personality, as in "What's in it for me?" (Service To Self) instead of "What is in the best interests of my group or tribe?" (Service To Others), several prevailing attributes of their consciousness began to characterize the way evolving humans saw themselves and interacted with other humans, including those within their own immediate community or tribe. According to Archangel Michael, several negative attributes need to be released before continued evolution into the Fifth Dimension of Consciousness would be possible; these include, but are not limited to, Fear of all types, Anger, Vengeance, Hate, Shame, Guilt, Judgement, Stubbornness, Indifference, Confusion, Rigid Thinking Processes, and Complacence.

Fourth Dimension: Sublevels 1-3. The Fourth Dimension of Consciousness is also the Astral Realms where a human's consciousness travels at night in their dreams. Sentient human beings within this stage of evolvement are still using some of their animal instinctual nature, along with the natural subconscious and conscious human nature. Therefore, the conscious energetic thoughtforms that inhabit this level are usually negative or self-serving, and can sometimes be remembered as nightmares.

Fourth Dimension: Sublevel 4. This is a transition area between the predominately negative and predominately positive energies that exist in the Astral Realm

Fourth Dimension: Sublevels 5-7. Energies and thoughtforms that exist in this area are predominately positive, and dreams of flying, lifting and rising are common, as well as dreams where the dreamer is fulfilling a positive action such as healing, teaching, building, mediating, etc.

Fifth Dimension. Archangel Michael reports that to fully enter the Fifth Dimension of consciousness, you only need to do two things: let go of all fear and let go of all judgement. When fear is released completely, there can be only love remaining; if all darkness is released, there is only light remaining. When judgement is released, only acceptance remains; when everything and everyone are recognized and accepted for what they are, there can be no better-than or worse-than, and only the most beneficial pathway ahead remains. However, the complete release of fear and judgement is the objective of the highest level of the Fifth Dimension, and Levels 1-6 are characterized by a steady and continuous letting go of the viewpoint of duality that characterizes the Third Dimension and integration of the qualities of unity and oneness with all of life. When there is unity and oneness, each individual recognizes and acknowledges the Divinity of each individual and life form, and all actions, words and deeds begin to emphasize cooperation instead of competition, one-ness instead of duality, and what is in the best interests of the group instead of separateness of individual beliefs and desires.

Again, there is no hard line of demarcation between Third and Fifth Dimension of consciousness; instead it is a continuous evolutionary process of letting go of Third Dimensional characteristics and adopting and integrating Fifth Dimensional characteristics with each person's energetic signature. Gradually and eventually, each person will become more and more Fifth Dimensional in their energies, and when each person's individual energetic signature becomes more than half-way (51%) Fifth-Dimensional, they can say that they have begun their continuing "ascension" process; when more than half (51% or more) of humanity can make that claim, The Collective Consciousness of Humanity will have begun its Ascension to even greater levels of awareness.

Dimensions 6-12. Although there are reported to be twelve Dimensions of consciousness within the Realm of Physical Form, the human brain and neurological system has not yet evolved to the point that it is capable of distinguishing between them or understanding at this time what the

155

characteristics of a physical body are above the Fifth Dimension of consciousness. In fact, there is no specific line of demarcation between these higher Dimensions; they blend together seamlessly, and, like the colors of the rainbow, one cannot say precisely where orange stops and becomes yellow, or where yellow becomes green.

We have, however, been advised that as we move "up" in frequency from 5D toward 12D, our physical bodies will become less dense materially, and will begin to become more light-filled or energetic. These higher energetic levels will also require that our physical bodies be adapted to be able to safely withstand the increased energy of the higher frequencies that promote and support our continuing spiritual and physical transformation. In one of the conversations with the Spirit Guide of the Channel, I inquired about the kind of changes we might expect as we continue to physically evolve as spiritual beings; the response was:

> *Humans' physical bodies will become lighter, lighter in density and lighter in being filled with the energy of Light. They will not experience disease and deterioration as they do now. The physical body will be the representation in physicality through which the Spirit is able to learn and grow, and experience Third Dimension in ways that help the entity learn. The physical body will not become such a concentration of focus that spiritual needs are ignored, but rather will be an assistant to that spiritual growth because it is no longer in need of as much intense care. It will survive more easily on more energetic foods and energies. There will be changes that reflect better health. The senses will work better; fewer people will need vision correction and hearing correction, etc. There will still*

be some who have chosen those lessons to deal in Third Dimension in blindness or deafness, etc., but those will be done more as choices, rather than as physical accidents or physical anomalies. The body will need less sleep and will have more energy in general and will seem to be more agile and strong to the entity as it grows, versus the density of bodies now which hold Spirit back.

I also asked if our evolving physical body is what some have called our "Light Body," and the Guide answered:

The "Light Body" exists within each human now, but it is what you may think of as "in the background". It is a part of each individual, but it is not the dominant body within that entity. Within third dimensional Earth, the physical bodies "override" the Light Body, as the physical needs are more in the focus and consciousness of the entity to deal with third dimensional Earth. The Light Body exists and as each human evolves forward, that Light Body can express more fully, until eventually the Light Body will be the main presentation and third dimensional physicality will be a choice by the entity. It will be as it is now for Fifth Dimensionals, in that moving into Third Dimension will feel like a heaviness, or a movement through thick liquid, versus light air, for that entity. It will feel like a "slowdown" or a "heaviness", and most will prefer to be within their Light Bodies most of the time. However, it will still require some sleep for rejuvenation. As the physical body advances forward toward being more in Light Body, it will need less repair because it will be enhanced by that energy from the Light Body. With that less need of repair, and less reconstruction needed, there will be less of a need for sleep where that reconstruction and repair is done. One of the important parts of sleep is to rejuvenate and repair. Another important purpose of sleep is to allow the mind to step back and the subconscious to review and organize and plan. So that also happens during sleep to sometimes resolve problems that the conscious mind could not resolve.

I asked the Guide if what we are calling the Higher Self of the individual is the soul of the individual; the Guides response was:

Essentially. The Higher Self is that part of each individuation (Soul) that presents in physicality and third dimensionality on Earth, yet when the physical body dies, the Higher Self survives and can move throughout higher dimensions, mostly staying within the lower twelve dimensions for experience. On Earth most humans have stayed within Fourth and Fifth Dimensions, moving back into Third Dimensionality when we separate dimensions. When we reach the state of becoming our Light Bodies, and that being our main presentation, we will be Fifth Dimensional for the most part. Once in Fifth Dimensionality, many things are possible for each individual, including things of which you are aware; telekinesis, telepathy, the manipulation of energy to create and to re-create physicality and energy presentations. Once Fifth Dimensional, you can play with Third Dimensionality, and create and rearrange matter within Third Dimensionality, but you also are able to move beyond that and create from a Fifth Dimensional perspective, which means that you can create from energies that are unavailable in the Third Dimension. Those [Fifth Dimensional] energies are much more malleable, much more open to what can be created from them, and are more "light-filled, bigger energies" is one way to describe them. They are energies that will allow that individual to move very far beyond what they have even believed to be possible. You would be able to locate your body in any place you wanted it to be, quickly and easily. Rather than having to travel from place to place, you could be at that place simply by wanting to be at that place. When you think of space travel from a Third Dimensional perspective, you think of getting into a space ship and moving through space for many, many Light Years to get somewhere. Those entities who now travel through space can travel in that way, but do not. For the most part, they are able to coordinate where they wish to be, and then move to that place. Once there, they can be visible and interact with what they find there, or (as around Earth now) can remain invisible and merely observe. Most of those ships that are in the skies above Earth now have "teleported" here. They haven't travelled through space over many years. They have arrived here based on their own wish to be here, and have come from wherever they came from via teleporting to the space the are in now.

I asked Archangel Michael to come forward and add anything else that he felt was pertinent:

Michael: *We have been trying to help you understand your movement into Light Body, as humans move forward into Light Body. They are mostly Third Dimensional at this juncture, but are opening themselves to become more and more Light-filled as the Light energies are poured onto Earth and onto those Humans. They are experiencing a flood within* *themselves of that Light Energy, and it is affecting their thoughts and their physicality, and their connections both to physical Earth and to Higher Energies. As these connections change from purely Third Dimensional physicality, they, along with Gaia as the Spirit of Earth, will become more pure Light Energy, more close to the original energetic Light that was poured upon Earth as Earth was created. Earth was created in ways that would provide Third Dimensional lessons that were unavailable in other energetic forms. The beings that lived upon Earth were given opportunities to move from very dense Third Dimensionality and Third Dimensional living, to move forward and still exist upon Earth, but be less dense, to become more and more Light Energy, and closer to their existence as their Higher Self. This is the change that has been occurring over millennia, tens of thousands of years for Human Beings, and they have reached a point, in coordination with a "Loop", a "Cycle" that provides more Light Energy for Humans as they pass through a photonic belt within space. As this Light Energy is poured upon Earth again, the humans who until this time have not been ready, are now ready to absorb more Light Energy. That Light Energy will change them in ways that will make it available for them to exponentially move forward in their evolution. They will be given the choices to do that, and can choose to not move if they wish. Most, we are seeing, will move forward, and therefore their bodies are changing, and will change more and more, and more quickly as they move forward now. Those bodies will become higher energetic bodies for them, but less dimensionally "dense" bodies. As Light enters each molecule, it expands and stretches and becomes brighter, which is the higher light, and the parts within that molecule are farther apart, so it is less dense. Therefore, it is more easily accessed for energy and for information than it had been before. Light Energy is part of energy that is received by the body and is used by the body to evolve forward. It is more easily done as the body is more Light-filled. As Light enters the body, it creates a more open space within the body for even more Light to come in, and this is a cycle that continues. As more Light comes in, it is easier for more Light to come in, until eventually the body becomes mostly Light, and is therefore very easily used by the Spirit itself, by the Higher Self. Physical bodies will definitely appear more Light-filled. They will definitely have a "glow" about them or have a very strong and visible aura that will be much larger than auras are around bodies now.*

That may be a lot to get our minds around right now, but the good news is that we don't even need to know how our individual and collective ascension will happen; all we really need to do at this point is to individually set our intention to continue evolving into the higher spiritual levels of awareness and existence that we came from, and our Guides and spirit Helpers will gladly answer our request.

Appendix C
Sharing Channeled Information

Our Spiritual Research Group (SRG) has been informed that intuitively derived and verbally channeled information and material should be appropriately used, managed and shared in a manner that is in the greater good of all those who originate, transfer and archive the material. Assuming that the information is given by or originated from highly evolved spiritual beings, they will understand what is of benefit for humans to know, and may even specify that certain information that is given to the Channel and Director should not be shared publicly at that time. As an example, when we investigated "Who made the Crop Circles, and why?" we were initially provided very direct and complete answers to both questions by my Guide, Michael, but were cautioned that the answers should not be shared publicly at that time. It was a full year later that we again broached the Crop Circle questions, and were told that it was then permissible to release the previously-provided information to the public if anyone asked us.

Sharing Considerations

Primary considerations for sharing information include whether or not the Channel and Director have given their permission to disseminate the information further, and whether or not either the Channel or Director desired anonymity. For our Spiritual Research Group, I have prepared a form on which I ask the Channel to specify the level of sharing of the information that they allow for each separate topic discussed during each channeling session on that date: Private (no sharing), OK to share within our Spiritual Research Group, OK to share within our Spiritual Discussion Group (SDG), OK to share with Leaders of other SRGs, and OK to share publicly.

Additionally, I ask the Channel to specify in writing whether or not they give permission to use the name of their Higher Self and/or Spirit Guide; in addition, the actual transcript of each channeled topic of discussion uses an alias or pseudonym to protect the Channel's physical anonymity. As the Director of all the hypnotic sessions for our SRG, I have no reason to hide what I do or say, so I do not insist on the use of a pseudonym. These procedures are in accordance with the guidance we received from one Channel's Guide when we established our SRG in 2014; her words of guidance, and those of my own Guide, Michael, were:

> *[**Channel's Guide**]: As you already understand, the first issue is that the individual doing the channeling gives permission for that information they have channeled to be shared. That is a small technicality that allows the channeling individual a sense of integrity and protection, especially in the beginning of the channeling experience. When the information is shared beyond the session and with the members of your Research Group, there should be some information about how the material is to be interpreted, in that it is information meant to assist in the understanding of the ascension process, that it is information meant to help the humans understand the world and the universe beyond their current incarnations, and it is meant to begin to help others open to their spiritual growth and journey. So, they should look to your channeling as further information, but not the complete story. There is more beyond, but this is a glimpse of what may come to help understand what may be going on, or has happened in the past, as a means of helping them begin to understand the expansiveness of the world they are moving into. And so, if that criteria is put forth clearly, then we might*

suggest asking the Group that, if individuals are interested in reading some of the channelings, that they contact you individually, they review a list of what is available, and you can provide them with that channeling with the understanding that it is not for publication beyond the Group because of copyright issues, et cetera. The concern about sharing beyond the Research Group is that once the information is released to the Spiritual Discussion Group in general, control of where that information goes and in what context is lost. Until another group such as yours has formed and had some of these experiences, they may not fully appreciate and understand what it is you are sharing or why. And in that case, misinterpretation could happen more easily. We are not opposed to the sharing once a group has been established other than your own, and has had the foundational experiences. Again, we are talking about developmental processes. The channels with whom you are working, and with whom you are developing the skill, have gone through experiential as well as spiritual experiences, have gone through a growth process that allows them the ability to understand and work not only with the processes, but also with the information that comes forth – of all kinds. And for another outside group to fully appreciate and make use of the channeling information, it would be hoped that they would have gone through similar processes of their own, and would therefore value what information you could share. It would seem that you and the Leader of a second or third Group would have conversations about this process that you are developing and would eventually enact. We would also like to add that we do believe that there are people currently in your Discussion Group who would benefit and enjoy access to some of the channeling information, and therefore, we do believe that in a controlled manner, information could be shared within your Group on a request basis, perhaps from a list of topics to begin with. We would also suggest that, as a preamble to the list itself, that you also discuss the limitations and concerns and use of the information before they choose. Michael and I have been discussing this as I have been talking with you. He has been contributing to the answers that I provided, and I have been summarizing the discussions we have been having as you ask your questions.

Howard, this is Michael. We do support that no personal information should be shared, from the soul development level particularly. That is protected and sacred information. However, information from the Akashic Record is discretionary, and perhaps the first decision-maker for that information should be the person who provided it in the beginning. Is it something they are comfortable with, to use your phrase, "your name on it?" We are very aware that our channelers of any kind and in any position also carry personalities and must function with those personalities and responsibility for their actions in a public arena. It is agreeable and acceptable to share the information, which is part of the reason for this Project. However, we are also monitoring the development of the Project and see where, at some point, the perspective, the sharing is going to be monitored by those like yourself with the integrity of purpose for the sharing. We believe that it is a work in progress that needs to be monitored carefully and cautiously at the beginning, and that when you actually have another Group – we have discussed this *before – that you and the Leader of the other Groups may have this dialog and this conversation about sharing information. We understand you are developing guidelines, and we appreciate what you have done – the integrity and the caring that you have involved in that – and we would like to see it continue as a model that perhaps, as you are developing the process of sharing, there be a statement to that effect, to the integrity and purpose, et cetera, of the sharing. For what reason are we sharing this information to begin with? Obviously, it is for enlightenment and education. However, knowing the issues of the human ego, it is possible as more Groups develop, for those understood issues to be lost in the process and eagerness to share information. So perhaps a statement of agreement as to why and how this information is to be shared, along with your permission slips, your written statements of the channelers to share, that those Leaders of other Groups also sign an agreement that their purpose for sharing and interchanging information is of the same purpose as yours. Obviously, because of free will, you cannot guarantee that they would not misuse their position; however, at least at a minimum they would be brought into full awareness of the issues and have to think about them and sign prior to any interchange of information. It is new – what you are doing – and it is coming at tumultuous and changing times, and we think it just needs to be a developed process and revisited from time to time as new events occur, such as the formation of a second Spiritual Discussion Group or new channelers come within your own Group. It is a child that you are raising, if I may use that comparison, and it must in younger stages be monitored and adjustments given as appropriate.*

*Make the intention clear as to the purpose of the
sharing, and be patient with the development of this
process. We are pleased with your progress and your
dedication to the work, and we are encouraged and
also celebrate with you the increased size of your
Group. I want to assure you that what you produced
and the direction you are taking is exactly what we
had hoped, and now it is time to release and relax, to
let us guide you and to communicate with us when
you have a concern. We are at a time when great
changes <u>will</u> be coming and may be coming rapidly
and create some confusions. That is why having
foundation groups such as yours where the aware, the
enlightened, can come and discuss what they hear,
what they experience, what their fears are, and to
share their own perspectives – that will help to keep
this energy balanced and grounded.*

To simplify and promote the sharing of written information
within our own SRG, and between other SRG as they are
established, several standards and protocols have been
developed for use in sharing the information derived by our
Spiritual Research Group, and fall into two categories: First, an
overall statement of intention of how the information in the
transcript extract of each channeling session is to be used and
shared; and Second, a written agreement and understanding of
how channeled transcripts may be shared between Leaders of
different SRGs.

First, to the edited transcript of each individual topic generated
from our SRG, the following notice is to be added: "<u>Note</u>:
This is a channeling extract from the Spiritual Research Group
Archive of Evergreen Healing Arts Center. LLC, in Chehalis,
WA, and is provided with the understanding that it is to be
used only for the purposes of assisting in the overall individual

and planetary ascension process, for fostering a greater understanding of our world and the universe beyond, and to help others open to their own spiritual growth and Journey. You should look to this extract as further information, but not the whole story. Copyright © (year) Evergreen Healing Arts Center, LLC."

Second, as additional SRGs are established, and wish to exchange channeled information with Evergreen Healing Arts Center, LLC, suggested formatting procedures for exchanging channeled transcripts will be forwarded to the prospective SRG Leader, who will sign and return a "SRG Leader Agreement" that will specify that the new SRG Leader has read and understands the information in the book, "*Spiritual Journeys: A Practical Methodology for Accelerated Spiritual Development and Experiential Exploration*," that they will be guided by the recommended procedures described below, and that transcripts of channeled information will be freely exchanged without regard to payment of any kind.

Recording The Session

To support convenient sharing of channeled information within and between established Spiritual Research Groups, commonly used data formats and convenient sharing procedures are recommended. The following standards and procedures are provided for recording, archiving and sharing information that have been adopted by my Spiritual Research Group; however, you are free to conduct your own SRG in a manner that best supports your SRG and SDG Members and Guests.

Each of our SRG channeling sessions consists of only the Channel and the Director. The session is conducted with the channel reclining in a comfortable recliner, and is recorded using a monaural Digital Voice Recorder (DVR) placed to one side about three or four feet away from the client's face. I use the sensitive or High microphone setting on an Olympus DVR Model 720, since it records the audio directly to a high-quality 48-kbps mp3 file, which is then transferred to a session archive folder on my office laptop using the DVR-to-USB cable included with the DVR. The file can then easily be transferred again to an external Flash Drive and given to the Channel as a record of their session. Flash Drives with a 4-Gb capacity are very convenient for this purpose, since they are close to the capacity of a standard single-sided DVD (4.7-Gb) and can hold over 150 hours of monaural audio when recorded at 48 Kbps. The cost of the 4-Gb Flash Drive is quite reasonable, about $5 each in quantities of 100. There are many internet vendors that provide a wide variety of Flash Drives, and many can also place your contact information and company logo on each Flash Drive as well. I have had very good results dealing with www.flashdealer.com.

Naming Your Recorded Audio Files

The entire original, unedited mp3 audio file for each channeling session is saved in the "Session Files" sub-folder of the "Local SRG Archive" folder on the SRG Leader's local computer for future reference, but will NOT be shared with my SDG/SRG Members or with the Leaders of other SRGs since the original file may contain personal information, or information that the channeled Source specifically requests that it not be shared.

The following naming conventions for the original, complete recorded mp3 audio files describe an audio file saved in the "Session Files" subfolder of my "Local SRG Archive" desktop folder as "2014-11-17 Karen Guardian Angels, Rosetta Comet Lander.mp3":

2014-11-17: Date the channeling session was conducted and recorded. This format allows files to automatically be sorted by date.

Karen: The pseudonym of the Channel.

Guardian Angels, Rosetta Comet Lander: The two main topics of investigation in that channeling session.

.mp3: The file name extension, which should be visible. If it is not, on Windows PCs, enter "Show File" in the search box on the desktop, then click on Show or Hide File Extensions, and make sure the "Hide extensions for known file types" box is unchecked.

Transcribing The Session

Once you have your session mp3 audio file saved on your computer, you can transcribe it to convert the information in the mp3 audio file to a text document file that is much easier and quicker to search than the larger mp3 audio file itself. *(Note: The complete original transcript file is never shared, and only edited extracts are made available for that purpose, as described later.)* Since there is currently no known transcription software that automatically converts spoken conversations with more than just one Source to text, you will probably need to manually transcribe your audio files. In addition, most transcription programs have difficulty with English language homophones such as their and there, eye and I, right and rite and write, site and cite and sight, etc. I use the "Express Scribe" software from NCH Software in Australia (www.nch.com.au/scribe) since it does not require a split-screen display on your computer (one screen for the text you type, and another screen for starting and stopping the audio playback). Instead, Express Scribe works in the background and gives you several "hot-keys" that you can use while you are typing in Word such as F9 to play, F4 to stop, F7 to move backward in the audio file, F8 to skip forward, etc. Express Scribe also provides for using an optional foot treadle to start and stop the audio playback.

A typical header for the complete transcription of the entire mp3 audio file for a single channeling session is illustrated here:

Guardian Angels, Rosetta Comet Lander
Directed by Howard Batie, November 17, 2014
Channel: Karen (a pseudonym)
Karen's Higher Self: Anaka
Karen's Guide: Joshua
Howard's Higher Self: Artoomid
Howard's Guide: Michael
Guest: Ascended Master St. Germain
Guest: (Others as appropriate)

Howard: Thank You, Joshua.... *etc.*

Text of transcription follows here with the speaker identified separately and bolded as shown.

The main subjects or topics of the channeling mentioned above (Guardian Angels, Rosetta Comet Lander) are in Arial font, 12 point, bold. All other information in the entire transcription is in Times New Roman font, 12 point, Normal. The date is the date of the channeling session, not the date of the transcription. The name of the person directing the channeling session is normally the name of the Spiritual Research Group Leader. The name of the Channel is a pseudonym to protect his/her identity. Other channeled Guests are identified if they contribute to the channeling. As an absolute rule, no personal information that would identify the channel is to be shared unless written permission is given by the channel to do so.

Note also that the specific channeled Source who provides the spoken narrative through Karen's voice is identified – in some cases the channel's Higher Self, and in others her Spirit Guide. My Higher Self and Guide are always present if I direct the channeling, and they may also be brought forward and directly addressed as well if desired. Additionally, for clarity and ease of reading the transcript, I use single line spacing with 0 points before and 12 points after each paragraph (carriage return) to separate the dialogue of each speaker; page numbers are at the bottom center of each page of the transcript. The edited transcript of the entire session would then be saved in the "Session Files" subfolder of the "Local SRG Archive" folder, as "2014-11-17 Karen Guardian Angels, Rosetta Comet Lander.docx" along with the original audio mp3 file with the same name, but with the mp3 audio file extension.

In addition, the Source providing the information may request that specific parts of the session not be shared with others. If that is the case, you must honor that request. Those portions which are not to be shared are printed in red.

Editing And Saving Transcription Extracts

A copy of the full transcription doc/docx file should then be made for further editing to remove any personal information. Further minor grammatical editing may be done to remove pauses and non-essential phrases that do not contribute to the overall meaning of the conversation.

Once editing of the complete transcript is finished, separate edited transcript extracts can then be made and renamed for each topic as shown below and saved as a pdf file in an "Edited Transcripts" subfolder of the "Local SRG Archive" folder. For the one topic of "Guardian Angels," the filename would then be changed to and saved as "001 2014-11-17 AEn Guardian Angels.pdf", and the "Rosetta Comet Lander" portion of the original file is renamed and saved as "001 2014-11-17 AEn Rosetta Comet Lander.pdf". If you have the Adobe Acrobat Reader Portable Document File application installed, the "Save As" options will automatically include the "PDF (pdf)" option.

[The Adobe PDF Reader application may be freely downloaded from www.adobe.com.] Each single-topic edited extract from the original transcription is the <u>only</u> item to be shared with other channels in your SRG, with other members of your SDG, and between SRG Leaders. Only the edited version of each topic's transcription should be shared, and then only in pdf format; this will make it more difficult (but not impossible) to modify or change the transcript's contents from the specific wording in the original session file.

The individual parts of the new filename are:

001: The SRG Number that originated the session, as shown in the "SJList.pdf" document that is discussed below.
2014-11-17: Date of the channeling session - this allows the files from each participating SRG to automatically sort by date.
AEn: 3-letter Language Code for the language in which the transcription <u>extract</u> is made.
Guardian Angels: Individual topic of investigation extracted from the original transcription.
.pdf: The Adobe Portable Document Format filename extension.

The language in which the written transcriptions are made (normally the language spoken by the Channel) must also be identified. All transcriptions of information developed by my Spiritual Research Group are currently in American English. As additional SRGs are established, the list of Country Codes will be expanded; however, to begin the listing, the following Language Codes are suggested, and can be added to as required:

AEn   American English
BEn   British English

Fre   French
Ger   German
Spn   Spanish
etc.

The complete format for the edited transcription <u>extract</u> for the single topic of "Guardian Angels" is provided below:

Guardian Angels
Directed by Howard Batie, November 17, 2014
Channel: Karen
Karen's Higher Self: Anaka
Karen's Guide: Joshua
Howard's Higher Self: Artoomid
Howard's Guide: Michael
Guest: (As appropriate; e.g., St. Germain, Archangel Gabriel, etc.)

<u>Note</u>: This channeling extract is provided with the understanding that it is to be used only for the purposes of assisting in the overall individual and planetary ascension process, for fostering a greater understanding of our world and the universe beyond, and to help others open to their own spiritual growth and Journey. You should look to this extract as further information, but not the whole story. Copyright © (year) Evergreen Healing Arts Center, LLC.

Howard: Thank You, Joshua.... *etc.*

Text of transcription follows here with each speaker identified separately and bolded as shown above.

Sharing Transcripts Between SRGs
Sharing of channeled information with others in our own Spiritual Discussion Group (SDG) is one matter, but it is entirely another matter when considering sharing our

information with others outside our SDG, and especially so if it involves sharing with interested parties in other countries. Assuming that the Channel allows it, sharing of their transcribed channeling sessions must also consider differences of language and vocabulary between the Channel and prospective readers of the information provided. Maintaining the integrity and accuracy of the original channeled information is of paramount importance. However, there are also many more mundane considerations to consider that could make the transcriptions easier to prepare, archive and transmit to other; these include style and formatting standards to ensure nearly the same "look and feel" of transcripts shared between Spiritual Research Groups (SRGs), for instance. The standards described below are those adopted by our SRG, and are suggested for consideration by other SRGs as they are formed.

As each new SRG is established, the SRG Leader should contact Evergreen Healing Arts Center (howard@howardbatie,com), and they will be provided with a link to the "SRG Archive" folder on my DropBox account. This folder contains three files: "Suggested SRG Procedures.pdf", "SJList.pdf" (the current listing of all SDG and SRG Leaders), and the current version of the Microsoft Excel "Consolidated Spiritual Research Index.xlsx" file. This Index contains a consolidated listing of all original session transcripts, and for which those individual topics have been made available for sharing by the originating SRG Leader. Feel free to copy or download all three files to your "Local SRG Archive" folder on your local computer. The format used for the Consolidated SRG Transcripts Index is illustrated in the below extract:

Consolidated SRG Transcripts Index			
SRG	Date	Lang	Topic(s)
001	2014-10-04	AEn	Nuclear WMDs, The Watchers, 5D Abilities
001	2014-10-30	AEn	Life On Mars, Message From Ashtar, Karma
001	2014-11-13	AEn	Time Slips, Do Guides Sleep?
001	2014-11-17	AEn	Guardian Angels, Rosetta Comet Lander
001	2014-11-29	AEn	Chakras, Mars, Disclosure, Crop Circles

This is a Microsoft Excel Spreadsheet that should not be "Sorted" to locate a specific topic of investigation; however, you can use the Excel spreadsheet "Home – Find & Select" function to easily locate subjects or topics of interest and to identify which SRG has a transcription extract made on that topic, the language in which the transcription extract was made, and when the channeling session was held. The SRG Number will lead you to the contact information of the appropriate SRG Leader, as identified in the "SJList.pdf" document. You will then be able to contact the SRG Leader who produced the transcript extract, and you may request that they email a copy of the transcript extract containing the topic(s) you are interested in to your SRG Leader, normally by attaching the file to an email.

For convenience and to save space in the "Consolidated SRG Transcripts Index.xlsx" listing, all the subjects or topics covered in a single channeling session are identified on the same line in the Consolidated SRG Transcripts Index; however, only the requested individual topic extract from that channeling session will be shared. Arial font with a size of 10 or 11 points is used for all information in the Consolidated SRG Transcripts Index. This Index will be maintained and updated as additions and changes are received by Evergreen Healing Arts Center;

however, it will be the responsibility of each SRG Leader listed to ensure that their information in this table and in the "SJList.pdf" file is accurate and up to date. Such changes, as well as updates to the "Consolidated SRG Transcripts Index.xlsx" and the "SJList.pdf" file, should be provided to howard@howardbatie.com.

The Spiritual Journeys Program and its development and procedures for archiving and sharing the information channeled from higher sources has been guided, directed and overseen by Archangel Michael as one method of sharing spiritual information that is seen as an initial model for collecting and sharing information in support of our continued individual and collective spiritual growth and evolution. Of particular concern is the development of information sharing procedures that can efficiently spread the channeled information while maintaining high levels of data integrity, as well as ensuring a clear understanding of the purposes for which the information will be used by each Spiritual Research Group Leader.

Additional Information

The Spiritual Journeys program is prominently highlighted on my website, www.howardbatie.com. There, you can find an excellent overview of the Spiritual Journeys goals and objectives, and I've also provided a 19-minute overview of Spiritual Journeys on YouTube.com; go to youtube.com, and in their search box, enter "Howard Batie" to view it.

Additionally, a 159-page "User's Manual" for the Spiritual Journeys program with over 20 case studies is available from Amazon.com; go to Amazon.com and in their search box enter "Howard Batie" and you'll be able to review a good portion of the book.

If you have any suggestions for improving these suggested procedures, please forward them to howard@howardbatie.com. I'm always interested in making it as convenient as possible to share the information our SRG develops within the guidance we have been given, and to also review the channeled information that other SRG develop as well.

Bibliography

Alexander, Dr. Eben, M.D., *"Proof of Heaven: A Neurosurgeon's Journey into the Afterlife"* (New York, NY: Simon and Schuster Paperbacks, 2012).

Baldwin, Dr. William J., *"Spirit Releasement Therapy: A Technique Manual"* 2nd Ed. (Terra Alta, WV: Headline Books, 2002).

Batie, Howard F., *"Healing Body, Mind & Spirit: A Guide To Energy-Based Healing"* (Woodbury, MN: Llewellyn Worldwide Publications, 2003). Voted by the Independent Coalition Of Visionary Resources as "The Best Alternative Healing Book Published In The US In 2003".

-------. *"Spiritual Journeys: A Practical Methodology for Accelerated Spiritual Development and Experiential Exploration"* (North Charleston, SC: CreateSpace Publishing Platform, 2015).

-------. *"The ETs Speak: Who We Are & Why We're Here"* (North Charleston, SC: CreateSpace Publishing Platform, 2016).

-------. *"Trans-Scalar Healing: Holistic Healing For Self, Others, & Gaia"* (North Charleston, SC: CreateSpace Publishing Platform, 2017).

Belhayes, Iris, *"Spirit Guides: We Are Not Alone"* (San Diego, CA: ACS Publications, 1985).

Benor, Daniel J., M.D., *"Spiritual Healing: A Scientific Validation of a Healing Revolution"* (Southfield, MI: Vision Publications, 2001).

Brennan, Barbara Ann, *"Hands Of Light"* (New York, NY: Bantam Books, 1987).

-------. *"Light Emerging"* (New York, NY: Bantam Books, 1993).

Brooks, Michael, *"Instant Rapport"* (New York, NY: Warner Books, 1989).

Brouilette, Dr. Michael, Ed.D., *"Changing Lives With Multilife Therapy: Getting the Most Out of Every Life You Live"* (Graham, WA: Multilife Publishing, 2016).

Cannon, Dolores. *"Keepers Of The Garden"* (Huntsville, AR: Ozark Mountain Publishing, 1993).

------. *"The Custodians: Beyond Abduction"* (Huntsville, AR: Ozark Mountain Publishing, 1999).

------. *"The Convoluted Universe"* Volume 1. (Huntsville, AR: Ozark Mountain Publishing, 2001).

------. *"Between Death and Life: Conversations With Spirit"* (Dublin, Ireland: Gill & Macmillan, 2003).

------. *"The Convoluted Universe"* Volume 2. (Huntsville, AR: Ozark Mountain Publishing, 2005).

------. *"The Convoluted Universe"* Volume 3. (Huntsville, AR: Ozark Mountain Publishing, 2008).

------. *"The Convoluted Universe"* Volume 4. (Huntsville, AR: Ozark Mountain Publishing, 2012).

------. *"The Convoluted Universe"* Volume 5. (Huntsville, AR: Ozark Mountain Publishing, 2015).

Clarkson, Joanne M., Hospice RN, *"There's Always A Miracle"* (Olympia, WA: Black Triangle Press, 2016).

Cota-Robles, Patricia, *"Divine Alchemy: We Are Becoming Crystalline Solar Light Beings"* (Tucson, AZ: New Age Study of Humanity's Purpose, 2016).

Elkins, Don, Carla **Reuckert**, and James **McCarty,** *"The Ra Material: The Law of One"* Books 1-5. (Atglen, PA: The Whitford Press, a Division of Schiffer Publishing, 1982).

Fiore, Dr. Edith, Ph.D., *"The Unquiet Dead: A Psychologist Treats Spirit Possession"* (New York, NY: Ballantine Books, 1987).

Flury, Matìas, *"Downloads From The Nine"* (San Bernardino, CA: Self-Published, 2014)

Foster, Jean K., *"New Earth – New Truth"* (Kansas City, KS: Uni-Sun Publishing Co., 1989).

Frankel, Edna, *"The Circle of Grace: Frequency and Physicality"* (Flagstaff, AZ: Light Technology Publishing, 2012)

Gamman, Tonya, *"Heaven and Earth: How It All Works"* (Issaquah, WA: New Swan Books, 2010).

Garfield, Dr. Patricia, Ph.D., *"Creative Dreaming"* (New York, NY: Ballantine Books, 1974).

Gerber, Dr. Richard, M.D., *"Vibrational Medicine"* 3rd Ed. (Santa Fe, NM: Bear & Co., 2001).

Glasson, Natalie S., *"The Twelve Rays Of Light: A Guide to the Rays of Light and the Spiritual Hierarchy"* (Pembroke, Dyfed, Wales: Derwen Publishing, 2010)

Goldberg, Dr. Bruce, *"Soul Healing"* (St. Paul, MN: Llewellyn Publications, 1998).

Hampton, Kelly, *"2012 And Beyond: The Truth from Archangel Michael"* (Bloomington, IN: Balboa Press, 2010).

Hayes, Janice, *"Ro-Hun Therapy: The Greatest Transformational Process of Our Time"* (Denver, CO: Outskirts Press, 2013).

Hayes, Patricia, *"The Gatekeeper"* (Durham, NC: The Dimensional Brotherhood, 1981).

Hernandez, Rey, JD, MCP**; Klimo,** Dr. Jon, PhD**; Schild,** Dr. Rudy, PhD, **[Editors].** *"Beyond UFOs: The Science of Consciousness and Contact with Non Human Intelligence"* Vol. 1 (San Bernardino, CA: The Dr. Edgar Mitchell Foundation for Research into Extraterrestrial and Extraordinary Experiences [FREE], 2018).

Hoodwin, Shepherd, *"The Journey of Your Soul"* (New York, NY: The Summerjoy Press, 1995).

Hunt, Dr. Valerie V., Ed.D., *"Bio-Scalar: The Primary Healing Energy"* (Malibu, CA: Malibu Publishing Co, 2008).

Hunter, C. Roy (Ed.), *"The Art of Spiritual Hypnosis: Accessing Divine Wisdom"* (Tulsa, OK: Blooming Twig Books, 2016).

Karagulla, Shafica, M.D. and Dora van Gelder **Kunz**, *"The Chakras and the Human Energy Fields"* (Wheaton, IL: Quest Books, 1989).

King, Godfre Ray, *"Unveiled Mysteries"* (Mt. Shasta, CA: Ascended Master Teaching Foundation, 2008).

Kuthumi, Ascended Master, *"Teachings For The New Golden Age"* (A channeled work) (Mt. Shasta, CA: Ascended Master Teaching Foundation, 2002).

Marciniak, Barbara, *"Bringers of the Dawn: Teachings From The Pleiadians"* (Rochester, NY: Bear & Company Publishing, 1992).

------. *"Earth: Pleiadian Keys to the Living Library"* (Rochester, NY: Bear & Company Publishing, 1994).

McHugh, Greg, CCHt, *"The New Regression Therapy"* (Lexington, KY: Self-Published, 2010).

McMoneagle, Joseph, *"The Ultimate Time Machine"* (Charlottesville, VA: Hampton Roads Publishing Company, Inc., 1998).

Milanovich, Dr. Norma, *"We, The Arcturians: A True Experience"* (Kalispell, MT: Athena Publishing, 1990).

Modi, Shakuntala, M.D., *"Remarkable Healings: A Psychiatrist Discovers Unsuspected Roots of Mental and Physical Illness"* (Charlottesville, VA: Hampton Roads Publishing Company, Inc., 1997).

-----. *"Memories of God and Creation"* (Charlottesville, VA: Hampton Roads Publishing Company, Inc., 2000).

Moore, Tom T., *"The Gentle Way: A Self-Help Guide for those who Believe in Angels"* (Flagstaff, AZ: Light Technology Publishing, 2006).

Moorjani, Anita, *"Dying To Be Me: My Journey From Cancer, To Near Death, To True Healing"* (Carlsbad, CA: Hay House, In., 2012).

-----. *"First Contact: Conversations With An ET"* (Flagstaff, AZ: Light Technology Publishing, 2013).

Newton, Dr. Michael, Ph.D., *"Journey of Souls: Case Studies of Life Between Lives"* (St. Paul, MN: Llewellyn Publications, 1994).

---------, *"Destiny of Souls: New Case Studies of Life Between Lives"* (St. Paul, MN: Llewellyn Publications, 2000).

Price, Rev. George Graham (aka Frater Achad), *"Ancient Mystical White Brotherhood"* (Phoenix, AZ: Great Seal Press Publisher, 1971).

Printz, Thomas, *"The Seven Mighty Elohim Speak"* (Mt. Shasta, CA: Ascended Master Teaching Foundation, 1986).

Reintjes, Susan, *"Third Eye Open: Unmasking Your True Awareness"* (Third Eye Publishing, 2003).

Reuckert, Carla L., *"A Channeling Handbook"* (Louisville, KY: L/L Research, 1987).

Ridall, Dr. Kathryn, Ph.D., *"Channeling: How to Reach Out to Your Spirit Guides"* (New York, NY: Bantam Books, 1988).

Rodwell, Mary, *"The New Human: Awakening to our Cosmic Heritage"* (New Mind Publishers.com, 2017; ISBN 978-0-9807555-1-0).

Schroeder, Werner, Ed., *"Man - His Origin, History and Destiny"* (Mt. Shasta, CA: Ascended Master Teaching Foundation, 1984).

-------, *"The Law Of Precipitation: How To Successfully Meet Life's Daily Needs"* (Mt. Shasta, CA: Ascended Master Teaching Foundation, 2000).

-------, *"Ascended Masters and Their Retreats"* (Mt. Shasta, CA: Ascended Master Teaching Foundation, 2005).

Selig, Paul, *"The Book Of Mastery"* (New York, NY: Imprint of Penguin Random House LLC, 2016).

Shapiro, Robert, *"The Explorer Race"* (Flagstaff, AZ: Light Technology Publishing, 2013).

Smith, Peter, *"Quantum Consciousness: Expanding Your Personal Universe"* (Warrandyte, Australia: The Consciousness Collective, 2015).

Stearn, Jess, *"Edgar Cayce: The Sleeping Prophet"* (New York, NY: Bantam Books, 1967).

Sugrue, Thomas, *"There Is A River: The Story of Edgar Cayce"* (New York, NY: The Penguin Group, 1942).

Talbot, Michael, *"The Holographic Universe"* (New York, NY: HarperPerennial, 1991).

Tolle, Eckhart, *"A New Earth: Awakening to Your Life's Purpose"* (New York, NY: Penguin Group (USA), 2005.

Woolger, Dr. Roger, Ph.D., *"Other Lives, Other Selves"* (New York, NY: Bantam Books, 1993).

Glossary

Angel: A spirit being whose purposes are to protect a human person from the danger of a harmful situation and to assist, if asked, in meeting the desires and needs of the person if their request is in the greater good of all concerned.

Archangel: A class of sprit beings who oversee the activities in the higher dimensional realms of the universe, whereas Angels do most of their work with incarnated beings. Archangels supervise and monitor aspects of events, and also work with the individual Spirit Guides. Archangels also assist, as required by the Guides, with souls who are in between physical incarnations.

Artoomid: The name the author's Higher Self has chosen to be known by.

Ascended Master: Spirit being who has experienced many Earth incarnations, has mastered all the lessons that physicality can teach, and who has elected to remain near Earth to assist in the ascension process of other individuals and of Mother Earth herself.

Ascension: Expanding into an even greater degree or level of learning and wisdom.

BP (Benevolent Prayer): A Most Benevolent Outcome said or wished for someone else. See MBOs and *"The Gentle Way"* book by Tom Moore.

CABG (Coronary Artery Bypass Graft): Surgical procedure that uses sections of a person's arteries (usually from their arm or leg) to bypass the area of a blocked or clogged artery supplying blood to the heart.

Calming Tool: A self-hypnotic tool that can be taught to nearly anyone so they can immediately release all feelings of stress and anxiety whenever they want. Great for panic attacks, presentation anxiety, test anxiety, and other stressful situations. If the person has received a formal medical diagnosis of "Anxiety," the Calming Tool must be provided under medical referral.

CH (Certified Hypnotist): A person who has been formally trained and Certified in processes and techniques to coach a person into a state of Hypnosis.

Chakra: An energy center within the human body. There are seven primary chakras whose function is to radiate the energetic vibrations of the physical body out into the universe, and also to receive similar resonating energies from the universe. A secondary chakra is also located at each joint between bones, and in the center of the palms and the bottom of the feet. See the author's book *"Healing Body, Mind & Spirit"* for a complete description and discussion.

Channel: A person who is able to connect with higher dimensional non-physical beings and transfer information that can be understood by humans.

Channeling: The process of transferring understandable information from non-physical beings to humans.

CHt (Certified Hypnotherapist): A person who has been formally trained and Certified in processes and techniques to coach a person into a state of Hypnosis, and whose ability and proficiency has been demonstrated in therapeutically assisting a client to resolve or release their negative conditions (such as emotional issues, pain and discomfort, weight management, addictions, etc.).

Collective Consciousness: See Group Consciousness.

CT (Computed Tomography): As defined by the Department of Health and Human Services, computed tomography (CT) imaging, also known as "CAT scanning" (Computerized Axial Tomography), provides a form of imaging known as cross-sectional imaging. A CT imaging system produces cross-sectional images or "slices" of anatomy, like the slices in a loaf of bread. (From Wikipedia)

Dimension of Consciousness: Archangel Michael's "Dimension" of consciousness may be thought of more as "levels" or "degrees" of conscious awareness. Although the levels of advancement have step-like names, each new experience bring an expansion of information, knowledge and wisdom in a continuous and gradual fashion that allows the consciousness of each individual to expand accordingly.

Dropbox: A cloud-based service that allows temporary storage and retrieval of document and image files via the Internet.

DVR (Digital Voice Recorder): A small, inexpensive handheld device to record and play back audible information. Some DVRs operate with their own proprietary format; however, one that operates with the mp3 compression format should be considered since this format is more universally used for sharing compressed audio files.

EHAC (Evergreen Healing Arts Center): The author's business identity in Washington State, USA.

EKG (Electro-Cardiogram): A medical device that monitors and records the electrical activity of the heart and provides a visual chart for interpretation by medical personnel.

Elohim: The Elohim are the first creation of The Creator as a method by which Creation could be disseminated in a variety of pathways and at a variety of levels. As a collective group of spirit beings (the singular is Eloha), they are responsible for the direct creation of the souls and life forms, following the directive of The Creator.

ESA (European Space Agency): The European Union's space exploration agency.

Exit Point: Situation, condition or time that the Soul may have chosen for the Higher Self to withdraw from the physical body and return completely to the Soul State, resulting in physical death.

Free Will: The gift of freedom by The Creator for all souls to experience whatever they choose to, without fear or judgement. All experience is a learning process, and the "Prime Directive" is to ensure that one's own actions do not restrain or constrain the actions or choices of any other sentient being. See also: Karma.

Group Consciousness: A collective grouping of several individual consciousnesses who have evolved to the same level or have a similar focus and interests and, therefore, have a similar vibratory signature.

Karma: The gift of Free Will permits any action or deed without judgement; Karma is the responsibility to experience the results of one's actions or deeds, either positive or negative.

LBL (Life Between Lives Hypnotherapy): The hypnosis-basis technique developed by the late Dr. Michael Newton that investigates the recalled experiences of each soul during the interval between physical incarnations.

MBO (Most Benevolent Objective): A very effective method of consciously enlisting the help of the Angelic Kingdom to assist in obtaining one's own wishes and desires. See BPs and *"The Gentle Way"* book by Tom Moore.

Michael: The name the author's Spirit Guide has chosen to be known by.

MRI (Magneto-Resonance Imaging): A medical imaging technique used in radiology to form pictures of the anatomy and the physiological processes of the body in both health and disease. MRI scanners use strong magnetic fields, electric field gradients, and radio waves to generate images of the organs in the body. MRI does not involve X-rays or the use of ionizing radiation, which distinguishes it from CT or CAT scans. (From Wikipedia)

Multi-Dimensionality: The ability to simultaneously observe and be aware from many different perspectives, levels of consciousness, or vibratory experiences (e.g., the physical body, the Higher Self and the Soul).

NASA (National Aeronautics and Space Administration): The American space exploration agency.

NDE (Near-Death Experience): The conscious recollection of having died, or of very nearly dying, and then returning to life.

Neurologist: A medical Physician who specializes in the study and treatment of disorders of the Central Nervous System (the brain and spinal cord) and the Peripheral Nervous System (all other neural elements, such as eyes, ears, skin, and other sensory receptors). (From Wikipedia)

OOBE (Out-of-Body Experience): An experience that typically involves a sensation of floating outside one's physical body and, in some cases, the feeling of perceiving one's physical body as if from a place outside one's body. (From Wikipedia)

PDF (Portable Document File): A file format developed by the Adobe company that is widely used for electronic sharing of printed documents and images.

PLR (Past Life Regression): A hypnotic technique used to recall memories of previous lives or incarnations. Past-life regression is usually provided by a trained Hypnotherapist as an aid in understanding and releasing negative emotions, feelings, or habits that may have their origin in a prior experience.

SDG (Spiritual Discussion Group): A group of like-minded friends and seekers who meet regularly to discuss and share their metaphysical experiences and related information.

Sentient Being: A conscious human or spirit being who is aware of its own existence and can feel, perceive or sense its environment.

SETA (Systems Engineering and Technical Assistance: Specialized contracted technical services that are provided to support the development, implementation and/or operational management of large civilian or governmental programs.

SJ (See Spiritual Journeys)

Soul State: A higher dimensional state in which all of the Soul's essence and energies are present and are not experiencing a physical incarnation.

Spirit Being: A non-physical consciousness; examples include those who have died and are in their Soul State, Angels, Archangels, Ascended Masters, Elohim, etc.

Spiritual Area: A state of expanded conscious awareness in which the practitioner is able to meet and converse with their own Higher Self, Spirit Guide, and other spirit beings.

Spiritual Journeys: The self-hypnotic program developed by the author to significantly accelerate the development of a person's spiritual and intuitive abilities, and to then use those abilities to explore the Physical, Astral and Spiritual Realms.

SRG (Spiritual Research Group): The Channels who, as a subset of the Spiritual Discussion Group, have learned through the Spiritual Journeys program to reliably channel spiritual and/or metaphysical information.

STO (Service To Others): A type of personal consciousness in which the adherents act in cooperation with others and in support the greater good of all concerned.

STS (Service To Self): A type of personal consciousness in which the adherents act in competition with others and whose actions and deeds are intended to support only the growth of their own personal power over others.

TNI (The Newton Institute): The organization established by the late Dr. Michael Newton to train experienced Hypnotherapists in the skills and processes of coaching clients through the Life Between Lives process. See www.newtoninstitute.org.

TSH (Trans-Scalar Healing): A purely energetic (non-hypnotic) healing technique developed by the author that teaches the practitioner how to develop Scalar healing energies within their own aura, rise into their "Spiritual Area" and provide a metaphysical healing session for others, regardless of where they are.

VAK (Visual-Auditory-Kinesthetic): The process used by Hypnotherapists to determine whether a person is most comfortable using visual, auditory, or kinesthetic words to describe their environment and experiences. See the book "Instant Rapport" by Michael Brooks.

Vibratory Signature: The energetic frequencies and vibrations of a spirit being; the energetic signature or "name" by which they are known to others in the spirit world.

Index

Notes

Notes

Made in the USA
Coppell, TX
12 January 2022